THE EXPERIMENT

BECAUSE EVERY BOOK IS A TEST OF NEW IDEAS

Also by Gill Rapley and Tracey Murkett

*Baby-Led Weaning: The Essential Guide to Introducing Solid Foods—
and Helping Your Baby to Grow Up a Happy and Confident Eater*

The Baby-Led Weaning
Cookbook

GILL RAPLEY and
TRACEY MURKETT

THE EXPERIMENT

NEW YORK

THE BABY-LED WEANING COOKBOOK

Copyright © Gill Rapley and Tracey Murkett, 2010, 2011
Illustrations copyright © Kate Larsen, 2010, 2011

The Experiment, LLC
260 Fifth Avenue
New York, NY 10001–6408
www.theexperimentpublishing.com

Originally published in the United Kingdom in 2010 by Vermilion, an imprint of Ebury Publishing/ Random House Group. This edition, which has been adapted and revised for North America, is published by arrangement with Vermilion.

This book is a work of nonfiction. Some of the names of people in the case studies have been changed solely to protect the privacy of others.

Many of the designations used by manufacturers and sellers to distinguish their products are claimed as trademarks. Where those designations appear in this book and The Experiment was aware of a trademark claim, the designations have been capitalized.

The Experiment's books are available at special discounts when purchased in bulk for premiums and sales promotions as well as for fundraising or educational use. For details, contact us at info@theexperimentpublishing.com.

Library of Congress Control Number: 2010934224
ISBN 978-1-61519-030-0
E-book ISBN 978-1-61519-131-4

Cover design by Alison Forner
Front cover photograph © Janice Milnerwood

PHOTO CREDITS: Pages 3, 5, 8, 25, 26 © Caroline Gue (of CP Photography); pages 17, 18 and 21 © Shaun Murkett; page 4 © David Payne. Thank you to the parents of these babies, for permission to use their photographs: Chloe Stanwick, 7 months (pages ii and 32); Arthur Gue, 6, 9 and 12 months (pages 3, 5, 8, 25, 26); Isabelle Dammery, 7 months (page 4); Santiago Baldessari, 6 months (page 9); Finn Warren, 6 months (page 15); Sophie Livings, 10 months (pages 17 and 21); Elsie Rweyemamu, 8½ months (page 18); Max Kellas-Mabbott, 10 months (page 20); Amy Spencer, 6½ months (page 24)

Neither the authors nor the publisher are engaged in rendering professional advice or services to individual readers and their children or relatives. The ideas, procedures, and suggestions in this book are not intended as a substitute for consulting a physician. All matters regarding health require medical supervision. Neither the authors nor the publisher shall be liable or responsible for any loss, injury, or damage allegedly arising from any information or suggestion in this book. The opinions expressed in this book represent the personal views of the authors and not of the publisher.

Manufactured in Canada
First printing January 2011

10 9 8 7 6 5 4 3 2 1

Contents

Introduction

Since writing *Baby-Led Weaning: The Essential Guide to Introducing Solid Foods—and Helping Your Baby to Grow Up a Happy and Confident Eater*, we've been thrilled at how the message about baby-led weaning has continued to spread. Families across the world have discovered that by starting solids this way they can introduce their babies to the pleasure of good, healthy food—and avoid mealtime battles later on.

If you haven't yet read our first book, and baby-led weaning is new to you, the first few chapters of this book will introduce you to the basics. With baby-led weaning, your baby's first experiences of solid food won't be puréed "baby food," spoon-fed to him by someone else. Instead he'll join in with family meals, picking up pieces of real food himself, feeling, sniffing and tasting them, and—gradually—learning to eat them.

Starting solids this way is easy, enjoyable, and stress-free. Preparing meals that your baby can share is quicker than making separate purées and cheaper than buying them ready-made. And it's much more fun. There's just one problem: The busy lives of 21st-century parents often don't include cooking traditional family meals, and many are short on ideas for healthy recipes that the youngest member of the family can share. This book solves that problem.

These recipes aren't the usual "finger foods" for babies, though. Nothing has to be cut into smiley shapes and there are no "hidden" vegetables. That's because with baby-led weaning there's no need for tricks. Your baby will enjoy the same rich variety of flavors and textures as everyone else—and he will learn new skills and grow in confidence at the same time.

The dishes are easy to make, tasty, and nutritious, but they aren't "ours"; they have come from other baby-led weaning parents who wanted to share recipes that worked well for them. They are favorite family meals, tried and tested.

If you've never cooked a meal from scratch before, or if you're not very confident in the kitchen, you'll find plenty of helpful tips to get you started. If you're already an experienced home cook, this book will provide inspiration for delicious meals that work easily with baby-led weaning.

We hope you enjoy sharing the recipes in this book with your baby and that they help to make family mealtimes the pleasure they should be.

Note: Throughout the book we have tried to be fair to boys and girls by alternating the use of *he* and *she* in the chapters. No difference between girls and boys is implied.

Part One

Baby-Led Weaning

"I love having my two children sitting next to me with us all eating the same food. I just make healthy meals and Elliot joins in—he'll try anything. There's no stress and he really enjoys it."

—Rikke, mother of Elliot, 11 months, and Ruben, 2 years

Chapter One

BABY-LED WEANING BASICS

Eating with your baby—at the same time, at the same table, and sharing the same food—is at the heart of baby-led weaning. There is no need for "baby food," purées, or spoon-feeding. Your baby simply feeds herself, exploring and enjoying healthy family meals, from her very first taste of solid food. Baby-led weaning (BLW) makes introducing solids easier and more enjoyable for the whole family and encourages your baby to become confident and happy at mealtimes and to enjoy good, nutritious food as she grows up.

The principle of baby-led weaning is based on the way babies develop and the skills that appear naturally in their first year. If parents give their baby the opportunity to handle food at about the right time, she will instinctively start to feed herself when she is ready. For most babies, this happens at around six months old, which is the same age when the World Health Organization recommends that babies should start on solid foods. The baby then progresses at her own pace, cutting down her milk feedings when she is ready.

This is very different from the conventional approach, in which the parents make the decision to start their baby on solids, beginning with spoon-fed purées and steering her through set stages toward eventually joining in family meals—something that often doesn't happen until well into toddlerhood.

Of course, babies helping themselves to family food isn't new; it's what babies seem to do naturally. Many parents, especially those who have several children, have spotted their baby grabbing something from someone else's plate and happily munching away on it. They quickly realize that letting her feed herself as soon as she can makes mealtimes easier and more enjoyable for everyone. For generations, parents have been encouraged to give their babies finger foods from six months onward, to help them to develop chewing skills. What is changing now is the assumption that babies need to get used to purées before they can move on to finger foods. This isn't the case. Sucking puréed food from a spoon doesn't prepare babies for chewing; the best way to develop chewing skills is to practice them on food that actually needs chewing—in other words, ordinary, unmashed food.

"We tried to start Thomas on solids by giving him mush—but he'd just clamp his mouth shut. He was so much happier when he could pick up pieces of food himself. He's always been a fiercely independent little person."
—Elizabeth, mother of Thomas, 13 months

Why Spoon-Feeding is Unnecessary

Most people still take it for granted that spoon-feeding is the normal way to give babies their first solid foods. But, like much of the current advice on introducing solids, spoon-feeding is left over from the days when parents were advised to start solids at three or four months of age—when their babies were too young to feed themselves.

We now know that babies don't need solid foods, and their bodies aren't really ready for them, until they are around six months old. If you've waited until six months to start solids with your baby, you've skipped the spoon-feeding stage. At this age babies are quite capable of feeding themselves, and they don't need to be spoon-fed. In fact, many parents find their baby of six months refuses to be fed by someone else; they want to handle food themselves because their instincts drive them to find out about things by testing them out with their hands and mouths.

"I gave Will some couscous for the first time today. It was fascinating watching him work out how to get it to his mouth. He seemed to learn a completely new skill in the space of one meal!"
—Karen, mother of Sam, 2 years, and Will, 8 months

What Happens with BLW

The first few months of BLW are not really about eating—they're about exploring food. Your baby will start by handling food, learning what it looks and feels like, then she'll use her mouth to discover its taste and texture. She may not actually eat any at first, but this is quite normal; her milk feedings (whether she is breast- or formula fed) are still providing almost all of her nutrition so she doesn't need anything else yet.

This is what happens typically in BLW:

- The baby is included in family mealtimes, where she watches what others are doing and is offered the chance to join in.
- Nobody "feeds" the baby; when she is ready she starts handling food and taking it to her mouth herself (at first with her fingers, and later with silverware).
- To start with, food is offered in pieces that are easy to pick up (babies soon learn how to handle a range of sizes, shapes, and textures).
- It's up to the baby how much she eats and how fast she eats it. It's also up to her how quickly she moves on to a wider range of foods.
- The baby continues to have milk feedings (breast milk or formula) whenever she wants them, and she decides when she is ready to begin reducing them.

Key Benefits of BLW

Going *with* your baby's instinct to handle food, rather than *against* it, makes weaning easier and more fun than doing things the conventional way—but there are many other benefits to taking a baby-led approach. It's great for babies because it:

- Allows each baby to move on to solid foods at the right time and pace for her developing body, and ensures that her important milk feedings are not cut out too early
- Helps to develop babies' hand-eye coordination, dexterity, and chewing skills

- Allows each baby to eat as much as she needs, in her own time, so establishing good eating habits that may last a lifetime (and which may help to avoid obesity and other food-related problems)
- Makes picky eating and mealtime battles less likely (when there is no pressure on babies to eat, there is far less opportunity for meals to become a battleground)
- Allows babies to explore the taste, texture, color, and smell of individual foods
- Encourages confidence at mealtimes and enjoyment of a wide range of foods
- Means babies can be part of family mealtimes from the beginning.

Baby-led weaning is great for parents, too, because it means more relaxed mealtimes for the whole family. There's no pressure to get your baby to eat and no need for games or tricks to persuade her to eat healthy foods. You don't need to make or buy purées, so eating in is cheaper and eating out is easier. Plus, of course, eating with those we love is an enormously important way of developing and cementing strong family bonds.

Is BLW Suitable for All Babies?

Some babies have medical or developmental problems that prevent them from picking up food or chewing it. Others, who were born prematurely, may need solid foods before they are physically able to feed themselves. If this is the case for your baby, she may need to be spoon-fed, at least at first. But, as long as it's safe, it is still a good idea to encourage her to handle food, to help her to develop some of the skills that she finds difficult. If you are in any doubt about your baby's general health or development, seek advice from a doctor or dietitian before you start offering solid foods.

"We decided early on that mealtimes were going to be a social thing, not just about the food. It really took the pressure off eating, and, now that he's older, Daniel joins in with our conversations, and mealtimes are just great."
—Lisa, mother of Daniel, 2 years

Chapter Two

HOW BABIES LEARN TO FEED THEMSELVES

Babies learn to feed themselves with solid foods naturally, when the time is right, but it can be useful to know when your baby is likely to be ready and how his skills will develop. This chapter explains what to look for and how you can help your baby to progress at his own pace.

The Right Time for Solids

For the first six months of their lives all babies need is breast milk or infant formula, which are full of easily digested nutrients and calories. Their digestive and immune systems aren't yet ready to cope with anything else.

Milk feedings continue to provide almost all of a baby's nutrition until he is about one year old, but from around six months he starts to need more nutrients than he can get from milk alone. However, the need is very small at first and grows quite slowly, so there is no reason to rush the introduction of solid foods. Most babies require only very small quantities of solid food until they are between nine months and a year old. They need time to get used to the feel and taste of food, and for their bodies to adjust naturally, before they eat more.

A baby's gradual need for more nutrients develops at the same pace as his skill at getting food to his mouth and his body's ability to cope with it. If he is allowed to feed himself from the beginning, he'll spend the first few months of family meals learning how to handle food (with his hands and his mouth), while his body gradually adapts to a mixed diet. So by the time he actually needs to eat more—between about nine months and a year—he will be able to feed himself a wide variety of foods, and his eating will become more purposeful. It's only then that he'll gradually start to cut down his milk intake.

Is My Baby Ready?

The World Health Organization currently recommends that babies be introduced to solid foods at around six months. At the time of this writing, the American Academy of Pediatrics is less clear: It says that most babies are ready to start solids between four and six months, but adds that they should be able to sit up by themselves and grab things to take to their mouth—which most babies cannot do before six months. A problem for parents is that many other "signs of readiness" they have been told about, such as waking at night and increased appetite, appear considerably earlier than this. We now know that these are not linked to the need for extra nutrients or the ability to digest other foods—they just happen naturally. If a baby needs fuel for growth, then calorie-dense breast milk (or formula) is the answer, not solid foods.

A few babies may be ready for solids a week or two before they reach six months, and it's not unusual for some babies to lack interest in eating until they are eight months or older. Most babies are truly ready to start exploring solid foods when they can do all of the following:

- Sit up with little or no support
- Reach out and grab things effectively
- Take objects to their mouth quickly and accurately
- Make gnawing and chewing movements

These signs usually appear together at around six months—rarely much earlier. But the most reliable sign is when your baby grabs food from your plate and takes it to his mouth and starts to chew it.

"I was peeling an orange one day and Rae was literally trying to climb out of her highchair to grab it from me. I gave her it, and she loved it."
—Lucy, mother of Natalie, 3 years, and Rae, 8 months

Moving Toward Solid Food

Learning to eat solid food is a natural part of any healthy baby's development, just like walking or talking. Skills gradually appear that are related to eating, but, at first, they have nothing to do with hunger. Babies take objects to their mouths because their mouths are extremely sensitive—it's a great way for them to learn about textures, shapes, and sizes.

By around six months, your baby's coordination will have developed enough for him to get things to his mouth more accurately, but he won't treat food any differently from his toys. He'll explore it with his hands and mouth, and he'll realize that it has a taste—but he doesn't know it's for eating. *He is curious, rather than hungry.*

Before long he'll discover how to gum and gnaw food, and then how to bite a piece off, although he probably won't be able to keep it in his mouth at first. Chewing comes next, but most of the food will still fall out of his mouth (so although your baby may appear to be eating, he isn't really). Chewing is an important skill; it softens

food and mixes it with saliva, making it easier and safer to swallow, and it begins the process of digestion. It's important for babies to have the opportunity to practice chewing from around six months to help them learn to do it effectively—babies who don't start chewing until they are older (ten months or so) often have difficulty with lumpy foods later on.

As his chewing skills develop, your baby will start to figure out how to move food to the back of his mouth to swallow it. This natural pattern of development means that babies rarely try to swallow anything before they have chewed it. Gradually, over a few weeks, less and less of what he puts in his mouth will fall out, and more will be swallowed.

"We offered Dylan some apple and pear for his first solids. We were so impressed with how accurately he managed to coordinate his hands to get the fruit into his mouth—he definitely wouldn't have been able to do that even a few weeks ago. He seemed to really enjoy it—not sure much was actually eaten though!"
—Louise, mother of Dylan, 6 months

The Gag Reflex

Many babies gag when they are learning to manage solid food in their mouths. It may be that this is a way of helping them to learn to eat safely, by teaching them not to overfill their mouths or to push food too far back before they've chewed it. Some babies gag only once or twice, while others continue to do it on and off for several weeks.

When a baby gags, food that isn't ready to be swallowed is pushed forward in a retching movement to prevent it getting to the back of the throat. In a baby, the gag reflex is very sensitive, so it is activated more easily than in an adult, with the "trigger point" much farther forward in the mouth.

Although gagging can be unsettling to watch, most babies don't seem to be bothered by it; they usually bring the offending piece of food forward fairly quickly, then either spit it out or chew it—and carry on eating quite happily.

To help the gag reflex work for your baby, make sure that he is sitting upright while he is eating (supported if necessary), so that any food that isn't ready for swallowing falls forward—out of his mouth—rather than sliding backward toward his throat. It's also important that no one but your baby puts food into his mouth, so that he can take the time he needs to control each mouthful effectively.

Although they are sometimes confused, choking is not the same as gagging; choking happens when something completely or partially blocks the airway (way past where the gag reflex is triggered). A total blockage is very rare (and requires standard first-aid measures) but babies can usually cough up something that is partially blocking their airway very well by themselves, provided they are sitting upright or leaning forward. Choking is no more likely with baby-led weaning than with spoon-feeding, provided simple, basic safety rules are followed. See page 27 for more information on safety.

Helping Your Baby to Learn

Babies need lots of opportunities to practice their eating skills and a range of foods to learn on. That way they can figure out how to manage different textures and gradually increase the amount they eat by themselves. There is no need for the traditional "stages," where you start with a few teaspoons of smooth purée and progress, eventually, to lumpy foods three times a day.

However, it is possible to pinpoint a few key eating skills that appear as your baby progresses, and this can be a useful way to make sure you are giving him all the opportunities he needs to learn and to widen his diet. Pages 11–13 identify what to look for and roughly how old your baby will be when these skills start to appear.

It's a good idea to prepare your meals so that they include textures and shapes that your baby hasn't quite mastered yet, alongside food he can manage fairly easily. Since most meals have a variety of shapes and textures, the easiest way to do this is simply to share all the different elements of your meal with your baby. As long as you include food he *can* manage, he will be able to try out the rest without getting frustrated. In fact, he will probably surprise you with what he can do, if you give him the opportunity.

Each skill will appear at the time that is right for your baby, so any attempt to teach him or push him is likely to be frustrating for both of you. He will learn to eat with a fork or a spoon eventually, but most babies find that fingers are the most efficient method for quite a while. If you concentrate on giving your baby the opportunity to try out different skills, he'll enjoy developing them in his own time.

"Eddie now wants to put a spoon in the bowl and get the food himself. He's always been pretty good at aiming with a spoon, but hasn't quite got the coordination to get it from the bowl yet—but he's on his way."
—Rachel, mother of Robin, 2½ years, and Eddie, 11 months

Developing Skills

Ready to start: From around 6 months

What you'll see	*Easy-to-manage foods*	*Foods for him to try*
He can take toys to his mouth accurately and quickly. He gnaws on them and makes chewing movements. He is able to sit up straight with little support and will probably want to join you at the table. He may grab a large piece of food from your plate and take it to his mouth.	Large stick-shaped pieces of food, including fruit and vegetables (see page 19), crusts, toast, large pasta shapes and soft meat patties or croquettes, shaped into "fingers." Long strips of meat.	See left.

Reach and grasp, with palmar grip: From around 6 to 8 months

What you'll see	*Easy-to-manage foods*	*Foods for him to try*
He can reach out for large pieces of food and grasp them, using his whole hand. But he can't get at the food once it's inside his fist, so he needs it to be long enough to poke out of the top, so he can gum or gnaw it. He may hold the food in one hand and use the other hand to guide it to his mouth. He doesn't yet know his own strength, so he tends to crush soft foods in his hands. In the early weeks most food falls out of his mouth because he hasn't yet learned to chew and swallow. He drops the food he's holding when he wants to pick up another piece because he can't yet release the food on purpose. He spends time examining food, passing it from hand to hand, and playing with it.	Large stick-shaped pieces of food, including fruit and vegetables (see page 19), crusts, toast, large pasta shapes and soft meat patties or croquettes shaped or cut into "fingers." Long strips of meat.	Foods for picking up in clumps, such as sticky rice, breakfast cereals, mashed potatoes, ground meat, grated cheese. Slippery foods, such as pasta with sauce.

Fist opening and closing: From around 7 to 9 months

What you'll see

He may be able to grab a fistful of food without too much squishing. Then, when he gets the food to his mouth, he can open his hand and push most of it in. He may also squeeze food into his mouth from his fist.

He will probably be getting better at biting and chewing. He may be happy to try a spoon or stick of food as a "dipper" for dipping into soft or runny food, or able to manage a spoon that has been preloaded with food by you. He continues to examine food closely and experiment with it.

Easy-to-manage foods

Stick shapes and clumpy foods, as on page 11. Smaller, soft foods, such as strawberries and chunks of cooked vegetables. Slightly crunchier fruits and vegetables (depending on teeth).

Foods for him to try

Runny foods to "dip" into, such as hummus, yogurt, thick soups. Sticks of raw vegetables for dipping. Different shapes of pasta, such as spaghetti or ziti.

Using fingers: From around 8 to 10 months

What you'll see

He may be able to use a "dipper" and pick up and hold pieces of food with his fingers, without having to use his palm. He makes careful selections of what to eat, and in what order. He may want to try using silverware, maybe even scooping food with a spoon or using a fork to try to stab whole pieces.

Easy-to-manage foods

Most stick shapes, clumpy foods and soft foods. Crunchier foods (depending on teeth). Runny foods, with a dipper.

Foods for him to try

Loose foods and small pieces, such as rice, peas, raisins, and crumbly breads. Smaller chunks of food for stabbing with a fork and soft foods to try scooping with a spoon.

Refined pincer grip: From around 9 to 12 months

What you'll see	*Easy-to-manage foods*	*Foods for him to try*
He can pick up very small pieces of food with the tip of his thumb and forefinger. He manages single grains of rice and finds the smallest crumbs! He may be starting to stab accurately with a fork and to scoop with a spoon. 　He may be beginning to play with food less and to eat larger amounts more purposefully.	Pretty much everything!	A full variety of textures and shapes, so that he can work out how to manage them with silverware.

Using silverware: From around 11 to 14 months

What you'll see	*Easy-to-manage foods*	*Foods for him to try*
He may want to use silverware most of the time, making mealtimes very slow. He probably finds a fork easier than a spoon for getting hold of food, but he may also prefer to go back to using his fingers every now and then.	Everything.	A full variety of textures and shapes.

Chapter Three
GETTING STARTED WITH BABY-LED WEANING

Baby-led weaning may be instinctive for your baby, but it is a different way of doing things for many parents. This chapter offers some ideas to help you get started and explains what to expect.

Eating Together

Babies of around five or six months are naturally curious and love to be included in any activity. So your baby is probably already letting you know that she wants to join in with mealtimes. She may not be ready for food quite yet, but she wants to know what the colors, noises, smells, and movements are all about.

At first, your baby may be happy to sit near you or on your knee and play with a spoon or a cup while you eat, but once she starts handling food it's important to make sure she's as upright as possible. In practice, this means sitting her either on your lap facing the table, or securely in a highchair—adjusting the straps and, if necessary, using rolled-up towels or small cushions to support her—so that she can move her arms and hands freely. And don't forget to wash her hands before she touches any food!

"It started off as a distraction technique really—I was trying to eat my dinner, and Morag wasn't happy playing with spoons—she kept trying to grab stuff from my plate. So I gave her some cucumber, just so I could carry on eating, but I didn't think she'd eat any. It was a week before she was six months. But she managed to get some to her mouth, and she seemed really happy."

—Lydia, mother of Caitlin, 3 years, and Morag, 12 months

Mealtimes as Playtimes

For the first few months of BLW, mealtimes are like playtimes for babies. This means they should be fun, of course, but also that, from your baby's point of view, they are a serious business—because it's through playing that she learns, develops new skills, and fine-tunes her coordination.

It doesn't matter if your baby eats very little in the beginning or if she misses a meal occasionally—this is normal. Both her nourishment and her hunger are still being satisfied almost entirely by her milk feedings (see page 16). The food you give her to play with should be nutritious, because she is learning about tastes and what to expect, but mealtimes aren't really about eating at this stage.

Sharing Mealtimes

With BLW there are no schedules to follow—you simply include your baby as often as possible whenever you have a meal so that she has plenty of opportunity to explore food and to eat when she is ready.

In the early months mealtimes don't need to coincide with your baby's hunger because she isn't relying on solid food for her nourishment; it's curiosity that makes her want to join in—she won't make the link between solid foods and a full tummy for a few months yet. In fact, as with any playtime, it's best to choose a time when she *isn't* hungry. It's also best to choose a time when she isn't tired; that way she'll be able to concentrate on taking in all the new sensations and practicing new skills. If she *is* hungry or tired she's likely to get frustrated and upset so, if she seems to need it, offer her a milk feeding (breast or formula) or let her have a nap before sitting her up at the table with you.

Some babies have very set routines and may be fast asleep at family mealtimes; others may still be having so many naps a day it's hard to see where any meals will fit in. If your baby is too sleepy to bother with food when you are ready to eat, it may be worth saving some of your meal and sharing it with her when she is more alert, then gradually changing either her nap times or your mealtimes.

When it isn't possible for your baby to share a mealtime with the family, make sure that someone is able to sit down to eat with her, so that she isn't eating alone.

*"Family mealtimes are great. We changed our routines so we could all eat together—
we eat much earlier now. And there's absolutely no focus on how much Mason is
eating—he's just one of us."*
                    —Vicky, mother of Alex, 3 years, and Mason, 11 months

What Happens with Milk Feedings?

Milk feedings (breast or formula) will continue to be the most important part of your
baby's diet until she is at least one year old. Solid foods simply can't provide all the
nutrients and calories babies need in their first year. So it's important not to try to
replace milk feedings yet, but to allow your baby to *add* to them with solid foods, at her
own pace, so that her diet becomes gradually more varied.

All you need to do is to carry on offering the breast or bottle whenever your baby
wants feeding, so she can decide when she's ready to start taking less milk. This probably won't happen until she is at least nine months old; then, as she begins to eat
more at mealtimes, you'll notice that she is beginning to reduce her milk feedings
herself. Some babies don't cut down noticeably until they are well past their first
birthday and many babies want more milk (and fewer solids) on some days than
others; there's no rush—your baby knows what she needs.

By the time your baby is about 18 months old she will be less reliant on milk
feedings, although if she's breastfed she may want to continue for another year
or more.

Offering Food

When you offer your baby food, it's best to put a few pieces in front of her, rather than
putting it into her hand for her. This way she can choose which piece to take first and
what to do with it—or, of course, whether to pick any up at all. If possible, offer foods
that the rest of the family is eating (as long as they are suitable—see Chapter 4), so that
your baby feels included and can copy you. She may "play" with the food by smearing,
squeezing, or dropping it; she may sniff it or take it to her mouth and lick it, but she
should decide whether she wants to actually eat any or not.

Most babies find plates and bowls just as interesting as food in the early days, and
will experiment with them to see what they can do. Although this is interesting for
your baby, it will distract her from exploring the food itself, so it may be better to offer

pieces of food on a clean highchair tray or tabletop, rather than a plate. (Or you can buy a special placemat, with a large pocket for catching dropped food.)

Offer just one or two pieces of a few different foods to start with, to prevent your baby from being overwhelmed. Keep some in reserve, so you can offer it later if she wants more. Remember to check that the food isn't too hot before offering it—tasting it is usually the most reliable way, especially if food has been microwaved, as this can produce uneven hot spots. Putting your baby's portion on a plate that has been in the freezer for a few minutes can be a good way to cool it quickly before serving.

Tastes

It's important to offer your baby a variety of tastes. Many commercial baby foods are bland or sweet but babies often like surprisingly strong-tasting or spicy food so, provided you avoid adding salt (see page 32), you can offer your baby plenty of different flavors (although you may want to go easy on the chili powder until you know how hot she likes her food!). That way you will be more likely to provide her with a wide range of nutrients and to encourage her to try new foods as she grows older.

"Fay loves food with plenty of taste rather than plain or bland food. She loves anything with lots of garlic or cumin especially."
—Lucy, mother of Fay, 14 months

Moving on to Silverware

Your baby will let you know when she is ready to try silverware. She may be able to dip with a spoon fairly early, but to pick food up she'll probably prefer a fork at first (provided it's not too blunt), because stabbing is a less complicated skill than scooping. Using a small, straight-sided bowl, rather than a rounded bowl, may make it easier for her to get something on her fork (because the food won't be able to escape as easily).

For runny foods, a small cup that your baby can hold in one hand (with a spoon in the other) will mean she can use both hands together. You may prefer to offer her a preloaded spoon to start with, so she can practice getting it into her mouth with some food still on it! (See page 22 for more information on runny food.)

Preparing Food for Your Baby

In the early weeks of baby-led weaning, the pieces of food offered to your baby should be a shape, size, and texture that she will be able to pick up easily. If you watch her you will get to know what she can manage, and you'll be able to adapt food quickly and easily as her skills progress.

To start with, your baby will only be able to grasp things with her whole hand, using her palm rather than just her fingers. She won't be able to open her hand on purpose to get at food inside her fist, so pieces of food need to be long enough for a bit to poke out and wide enough for her to grab and close her fingers around. Thick sticks and strips are ideal. She won't be able to get hold of anything small, so think big.

Once she's got going with BLW, your baby will enjoy learning how to handle other shapes and textures. Offering foods such as rice, pasta, and ground meat (and even soup) alongside pieces of food she can pick up easily (see pages 11–13) will allow her to experiment and explore without getting too frustrated. Most babies are very inventive, and the more experience your baby has with foods that need different kinds of handling and chewing, the more quickly she'll learn to deal with them.

Vegetables

Vegetables such as green beans, asparagus, and snow peas just need to be trimmed, while broccoli and cauliflower work well as florets—with a bit of stalk to provide a "handle." Potatoes, sweet potatoes, and squashes are best cut into sticks or wedges, with some skin left on. Other large vegetables should be cut into thick stick shapes—roughly 2 inches long and ½ to ¾ inches wide.

Vegetables can be steamed, boiled, grilled, roasted, stir-fried, or baked. They should be firm enough for your baby to hold but soft enough for her to munch, so if you usually like your vegetables with a bit of "bite" (al dente), you may find that you need to cook them a little longer, especially if she hasn't got any teeth yet. If you cook small vegetables (such as peas) until they're soft, your baby may be able to squash together a fistful even though she can't yet pick them up on their own.

"If we have a stir-fry I'll make sure there are some big bits and just put some of them on Luke's tray. He especially enjoys whole baby corn and snow peas."
—Sharon, mother of Luke, 10 months

Salad Vegetables

Cucumber can be cut into sticks and raw bell peppers into thick strips; celery should have the coarse strings removed. Lettuce can be offered in strips or as rolled-up leaves (although your baby is unlikely to be able to chew it effectively, she'll probably want to try). Tomatoes are usually easier for babies to deal with if halved or quartered (depending on their size); cherry tomatoes should be cut in half.

Fruit

Fruit is easier to hold when it's left unpeeled because it is less slippery. Later, when they can bite chunks off, some babies find the peel of fruits such as apples difficult to chew. Watch your baby to judge what's best. And don't worry about skin that isn't meant to be eaten (such as pineapple)—she'll soon work out which bits are edible. All fruit should be washed and any pits removed.

You can offer your baby apples and pears in halves or quarters (not in small pieces), or you can leave the fruit whole. If you do leave it whole, you may want to remove the core, so that your baby can put her thumb inside to help her hold it. Choose softer varieties, which are less likely to break off in hard chunks (microwaving hard apples for a few

seconds softens them). Taking a bite out of the fruit yourself first will help your baby to get started.

Fruits such as avocado, pineapple and melon are best cut into wedges; nectarines and apricots can be offered in halves or quarters. Blueberries should be crushed slightly and grapes should be cut in half. Soft berries such as strawberries and raspberries can be offered whole —your baby will enjoy learning how to hold them without crushing them.

Bananas can be offered whole but they are usually too wide for small hands to grasp easily, so it's best to cut them lengthwise. If the banana is nice and ripe, try putting pressure on the top end with your finger—it should fall naturally into three long sections, which you can then cut in half. Alternatively, cut the banana in half and trim the skin back, so that the top sticks out like ice cream in a cone.

"Ellen will chew away at an apple slice and then just spit out the skin."
—Joanne, mother of Isabella, 2 years, and Ellen, 8 months

Pasta

Forget "baby" pasta—your baby won't be able to get hold of it yet—instead go for large pieces that she can hold with her whole hand. Twisty shapes are easier to grasp than straight shapes, and sauces stick better to them, too—try fusilli and rigatoni in the beginning, moving on to smaller and smoother shapes as your baby's skills develop. Spaghetti is great fun, but you may want to save it for when you have plenty of time for the cleaning up! It's best not to add oil to your pasta when cooking it because it makes it slippery. At first your baby may prefer pasta served plain, with a little sauce on the side to play with or to lick off her fingers. Once she is more experienced with food, she will be able to manage pasta and sauce together.

Rice

Ordinary long-grain rice may be tricky for your baby to manage in the very early days, although rice that has been slightly overcooked tends to stick together quite well. A better alternative is sticky rice or sushi rice, or you may want to start with dishes such as risotto (see pages 136–139), which can be picked up in soft handfuls, or onigiri (see page 63). Later, your baby will enjoy picking up individual grains.

"If we have rice I'll mix it with a sauce so it's a bit stickier and put it on a spoon, and then just put the spoon in front of Micky so he can feed himself with it. It's very messy but he really likes it."
—Rosy, mother of Will, 2 years, and Micky, 11 months

Meat

Babies often enjoy sucking or gnawing on meat as soon as they start solid food. It is best offered in large strips or on the bone. Lamb, beef, and pork need to be cooked so that the meat is very tender (stewing or slow cooking is good, whereas grilling can make it more chewy). Small homemade patties or burgers are easy to handle, and after the first few weeks your baby will probably be able to pick up fistfuls of ground meat, too. If you offer your baby sausages, remove the skin first.

Chicken is easy for babies to manage. Tear strips of breast meat along the grain, rather than across, so that they stay in one piece. Thigh meat tends to be juicier and firmer than breast, while drumsticks are ideal for small hands. Remember to remove any thin splint bones or loose gristle first.

Bread

Most babies find bread easier to manage if it is toasted—soft white bread in particular can stick to the roof of a baby's mouth. Flat breads, such as pita, tortilla wraps, and chapatis, are also easier to manage than "ordinary" bread. Toast and bread can be cut into finger shapes, strips, or small triangles.

Other Foods

Many other nutritious foods (see Chapter 4) can be adapted easily for your baby in the early weeks—offer whatever you think she can manage. Homemade fishcakes, meatballs, and patties can be made in easy-to-handle shapes, and hard cheeses, such as Cheddar, can be cut into sticks. Offer your baby a variety of shapes, sizes, and textures as she progresses, but don't forget to include some easy shapes with most meals while she is learning.

Runny Foods

Runny foods can be adapted so that your baby can manage them. Soups and hot breakfast cereals are easy to make extra thick, and soups can have rice, small pieces of bread, or tiny pasta shapes added to them so that your baby can scoop up handfuls. Bread or dumplings can be served with soups and stews, while cooled smooth soups (and yogurt) can be "drunk" from a cup.

From about eight months your baby may be able to use a dipper, such as a breadstick or stick of carrot, with runny or soft foods. A piece of celery is especially good for scooping up dips. Alternatively, you could offer her a preloaded spoon to hold.

Drinks

Once your baby has joined you for meals, it's a good idea to offer her water in a small open cup (a shot-glass size is ideal) whenever she sits down to eat. She'll probably just want to play with it at first, but if she needs it, she'll let you know, and you can help her hold it steady for drinking if necessary.

Buying a highchair

The most useful highchairs are those that come right up to the table, so that your baby can feel truly included in family mealtimes. Many can be adjusted for older children and are a good long-term investment. If you opt for one with a tray, make sure it is fairly wide with adjustable tray positions so your baby can reach her food comfortably (many highchairs are toddler-sized, with a fixed tray position). An adjustable footrest will also make her more stable and help her to feel secure.

You'll probably want to think about how easy a highchair is to clean, too. Simple wooden or plastic highchairs are much easier to clean than those with lots of padding—and if it has a tray, make sure it's detachable so it can be washed in the sink.

Trusting Your Baby's Appetite

Babies are able to decide how much they need to eat, but their appetites can vary from day to day. Some days your baby will eat a lot, while on other days she may peck at her food or not want to eat anything solid at all. This is entirely normal and, as long as she is well, you are offering a variety of healthy foods, and she is able to have as many milk feedings as she wants, she will be well nourished.

If—once she's eating purposefully—your baby refuses food, it could be because she's teething, coming down with a cold, or simply feeling upset (for example, in the first few days after her mother or father returns to work). Some babies (and children) regularly eat a lot for a few meals and then very little for the next few days—it's just their natural pattern.

It's important not to push your baby to eat more than she wants. If you were brought up to believe children should clean their plate, offering her a very small portion (with more available if she wants it), may help you to resist coaxing her into eating more than she needs. Your baby is the only person who knows how much is enough.

"Remembering not to battle about food was harder as Joshua got older. I had to remember not to bully him and remind myself that he's good at self-regulating and he'll only eat what he wants, so trying to persuade him to eat more never works."
—Sue, mother of Joshua, 3 years

Knowing when She's Finished Eating

Babies have their own ways of telling their parents they've finished eating, and you'll soon learn to interpret your baby's signals. She may look bored, begin playing with her bib or a squashed bit of food, or start wriggling to get down. Dropped food can be a useful sign; young babies drop food by accident, but once they have learned to do this on purpose (usually at around nine or ten months), repeated dropping of food generally means that they have lost interest in the meal. Some babies simply push food away from them or make sweeping movements across their tray or the table. If you're not sure what your baby is trying to tell you, offer her a little more (perhaps a different taste) and see how she responds.

"Mabel is an incredibly efficient communicator at mealtimes. Now, when she finishes something, she hands it to me and shakes her head; she'll only start dropping things when we haven't been listening properly. Yesterday she had some falafel she didn't want, so she handed it to me and shook her head. But

her dad hadn't noticed this, saw no falafel on her plate, and put some on. She just dumped it straight on the floor, which is totally understandable."

—Rae, mother of Mabel, 1 year

Snacks and Food on the Move

Until she is at least nine months old, your baby's main between-meal "snack" should normally be a milk feeding. Once her appetite for other foods really kicks in (which may not be much before she's a year, or even later), making sure you have a healthy snack with you when you are out and about will mean you can avoid buying highly processed foods and sweets to fill a hunger gap.

Snacks are an important part of a child's diet, so think of them as mini meals rather than as "extras." If the snack is nutritious, it doesn't matter if it "spoils her appetite" for the next meal. Young children need to eat little and often.

Simple Snack Ideas

Snacks are really just foods that you can give to your child quickly and easily, whenever they are needed. Healthy baked snacks such as homemade muffins, scones (see page 164) and oat bars (see page 169) are ideal to make in batches and have ready, but there are plenty of foods that will make perfect snacks that you may already have in the house:

- Fruit, served whole or as slices
- A handful of dry cereal (low-sugar, low-salt variety)
- Rice cakes, toast, or bread with spread
- A piece of cheese
- Strips of cooked meat or a chicken drumstick
- Leftover cooked vegetables (such as whole baby corn, snow peas or snap peas, green beans, or sticks of carrot or zucchini)
- Leftovers such as slices of frittata (see page 120), homemade pizza (see page 127), or portions of cold pasta dishes

What to Expect with BLW

Although some things will be the same however you introduce solids to your baby, many aspects of baby-led weaning are quite different from conventional weaning. Here are some things you can expect over the first few months.

Mess!

There's no denying that baby-led weaning can be very messy indeed at the beginning, but the messy phase tends to be short. In the meantime, a clean plastic mat under your baby's chair will protect the floor and allow pieces of food to be safely handed back.

Try to avoid the temptation to wipe your baby's face or hands while she's handling food; it will be annoying for her, and interrupt her concentration and fun. Saving bath time until after dinner is a good idea, too.

If you are eating at someone else's house you can take your splash mat, or an old newspaper, with you. You could also take along some nonrunny food for your baby, so you'll have something else to offer if the meal looks as though it could be very messy.

Overall, it's important to allow your baby to explore food freely as much as possible both for learning and enjoyment—even if she does make a bit of a mess.

Longer Mealtimes

Be prepared to allow your baby plenty of time to learn new skills and to find out about food. Chewing can be a slow business at first, but learning to chew effectively is essential for good digestion and to minimize the chance of choking. Hurrying your baby—or trying to "help" her—will distract her and may delay her progress.

Changing Poop

When your baby starts eating solid foods, her poop will change. In fact, the best way of knowing whether your baby is actually swallowing any food in the early days is by what you see in her diaper. If she has managed to swallow some food, her poop will contain "bits." Some may look almost the same as when they went in; this is normal and simply reflects her developing chewing skills. Over the next few months, as she begins to eat more and to chew more effectively, you'll notice her poop will become darker, smellier, and more solid.

> *"Felix loves cooked beets (with no vinegar), and he'll eat loads. But they go straight through him and make his poop dark red or purple!"*
>
> —Tom, father of Felix, 2 years

Getting Frustrated

Sometimes babies go through a phase of appearing frustrated with food. This is similar to the frustration that sometimes happens with a new toy; it isn't caused by your baby needing (and not being able to eat) the food she's trying to get to her mouth, it's simply impatience at skills that are developing more slowly than she would like. So there's no need to spoon-feed her or put the food in her mouth for her; the frustration won't last long if she's allowed to work it out for herself.

However, before you decide that your baby is just a bit frustrated, check the following:

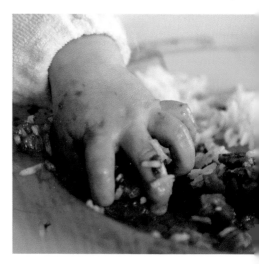

- Is she tired or hungry? Babies can change their feeding and sleeping patterns without warning, so today may not be the same as yesterday.
- Is she comfortable and able to reach the food easily? She may need a bit of extra support so she can lean forward.
- Are the pieces of food the right size and shape for her to grasp? Or, if she is older and is finding a new skill difficult (such as picking up peas), does she have some pieces of food that she can easily manage alongside the tricky ones?
- Would she prefer to sit on your lap for a few meals, to help her to feel more confident?

Food Choices

Babies and small children occasionally want to eat nothing but one particular food, sometimes for several days at a time. These unpredictable food "fads" are quite normal. Just continue to offer your baby varied, healthy meals and let her choose from them what she wants to eat—even if her diet doesn't seem particularly well balanced on the day, it will probably even out over the course of a week or so.

If your baby rejects a particular food it doesn't necessarily mean she doesn't like it. It probably means she doesn't want or need that food at that time. If it's something you serve regularly, carry on offering it—she'll probably change her mind in a few days.

BLW basics

- Offer food at times when your baby isn't tired or hungry.
- Allow your baby to explore food and play with it.
- Start by offering foods that are easy to pick up—preferably the same as those you are eating.
- Offer a variety of foods throughout the week, with different tastes and textures, avoiding foods that aren't nutritious.
- Don't expect her to eat very much for the first few months. Her appetite for solid food will probably start to increase anytime from around nine months to a year.
- Carry on offering breast milk or formula feedings. Expect your baby's milk-feeding pattern to change only very gradually as she starts to eat more.
- Don't hurry your baby or distract her while she is handling food, or try to persuade her to eat more than she wants.
- Offer your baby water with her meals, in case she is thirsty.

Keeping mealtimes safe

- Make sure your baby is sitting upright to eat, not leaning back or slumping.
- Keep whole nuts out of your baby's reach.
- Offer larger fruits, such as apples, whole or cut into big pieces; cut small fruits such as grapes and cherries in half and remove any pits or seeds.
- Remove skins from sausages, and gristle and small bones from meat and fish.
- Don't let anyone except your baby put food into her mouth—including "helpful" older children.
- Explain how baby-led weaning works to anyone caring for your baby.
- NEVER leave your baby alone with food.

Gagging

Don't be surprised if your baby gags occasionally when she starts feeding herself with solid foods. This is quite normal (see page 9) and is not the same as choking—it's just a way of pushing forward food that needs a bit more chewing. For some babies, gagging leads to a small vomit. However, although it can be a bit disconcerting to watch, it doesn't seem to bother them—and it happens less and less often as they learn to control food in their mouths more effectively.

If your baby starts to gag, make sure she is sitting upright or leaning slightly forward, so that the food she's trying to move can fall out of her mouth, rather than going back toward her throat. Slapping her on the back won't help her (and may make her more likely to choke), so try to stay calm while she deals with it, and smile at her once she's sorted it out.

> *"Every time Amy gagged I was ready to jump up and flip her over but once I got used to letting her have that extra few seconds she'd deal with it and be halfway through the next mouthful of food by the time I'd recovered!"*
>
> —Emily, mother of Amy, 6 months

Gradual Progress

Each baby is different, and baby-led weaning allows them to develop their eating skills at their own unique pace, rather than in clear "stages" (as with conventional weaning). As with any new skill your baby learns, it will probably be two steps forward and one step back. For example, she may start using silverware for a couple of weeks and then go back to using her fingers for a month or two. All of this is normal. In fact, as your baby progresses with baby-led weaning, it's likely that her abilities will take you by surprise as she gradually becomes more and more accomplished at mealtimes.

Chapter Four
WHAT TO EAT

Baby-led weaning is all about sharing healthy family food with your baby; most food that is good for you is good for your baby, too. So as long as you offer a varied, balanced diet that is made up mainly of fresh and healthy ingredients, and avoid the few foods babies shouldn't have, you won't go wrong—and your baby will be well on the way to developing a taste for nutritious meals that will help him to make sensible food choices when he is older.

A Healthy Diet

A healthy diet for the whole family is one that provides all the necessary nutrients in roughly the right proportions, and gives you all plenty of energy. In the first few months of solids there's no need to worry about balancing the different types of food for your baby because he is still just exploring; his milk feedings (breast milk or formula) contain all the nutrients he needs. And, unless there are allergies in the family, there's no need to introduce foods one at a time (as parents used to be advised to do) because by six months babies' digestive and immune systems can cope with a wide variety of foods. If your baby shares healthy meals with you, as soon as he does begin to need extra nutrients they will be readily available for him.

We find it useful to think of food in four main categories: fruits and vegetables, carbohydrate-rich foods, protein-rich foods, and calcium-rich foods, plus a fifth, smaller group—fats. Adults (and older children) should aim to have plenty of carbs, with smaller amounts of protein foods, calcium-rich foods, and a small amount of fat. Babies' needs are slightly different (see page 30), although having five fruits and vegetables a day and eating fish at least twice a week is good advice for both babies and adults.

Food Groups

Fruits and vegetables provide important vitamins and minerals. Try to offer as many differently colored fruits and vegetables as you can—they all provide different nutrients.

Carbohydrate-rich foods provide energy, and many also contain protein, as well as some important vitamins and minerals. Examples are wheat, rice, oats, and other grains (and foods made from them, such as bread and pasta), as well as starchy vegetables such as potatoes and yams.

Protein-rich foods are vital for growth. Meat, fish, eggs, and cheese are all full of protein and are excellent foods for babies. Tofu and quinoa are the highest plant sources of protein, while dried beans and legumes (such as beans, chickpeas, and lentils) and nuts are also protein-rich.

Calcium-rich foods include dairy foods, such as milk, cheese and yogurt, tofu, sesame seeds (for example as in tahini), almonds, and canned fish with soft, edible bones, such as sardines.

Fats provide energy in a concentrated form. Some fats are important for the healthy functioning and development of the brain. They are found in good quantities in fish (especially oily fish), avocados, nuts, and seeds. Fats are also plentiful in meat, eggs, and dairy foods. Adults shouldn't have too many saturated fats (mainly animal fats, from meat, cheese, and butter) and the whole family should avoid trans-fats, or fats that have been hydrogenated (as contained in some margarines, and normally used in store-bought pies, cookies and cakes).

"When Kyle was eight or nine months he loved dark green vegetables like Brussels sprouts—in fact anything with lots of vitamin C he seemed to go for first."
—Linda, mother of Kyle, 16 months

Extra Needs for Babies

Babies and young children need more fat and calcium than adults. Breast milk and infant formula contain plenty of these important nutrients, but as babies gradually start to have less breast milk or formula (usually from about nine months onward), they need to get fat and calcium from the rest of their diet in order to grow and develop healthily. So although a low-fat diet may be better for their parents and older siblings, children under two years old, who aren't relying on milk feedings, should have full-fat dairy foods (milk, yogurt, butter, and cheese) to ensure that they get all the nutrients and energy they require. Oily fish with edible bones are a good source of both fat and calcium.

Iron and zinc are the first nutrients that babies start to need in addition to those provided by breast milk. Most babies are born with stores of these minerals to last them well beyond six months, but it's a good idea to offer foods that contain them early on, so that your baby can help himself to them as soon as he needs them. Most foods that are rich in iron are also good sources of zinc. Slow-cooked meat (especially beef) is the best source, and fish and eggs also provide plenty. Tofu, dried beans and legumes, and dark green leafy vegetables contain good amounts of iron (and zinc)—although it's not as easily absorbed as it is from animal sources. In North America, much bread, wheat flour, and many breakfast cereals are fortified with iron. Eating foods that contain vitamin C (most vegetables and fruit) at the same meal as iron-rich foods helps to maximize iron absorption—even a squeeze of lemon juice makes a difference. (See page 38 for specific information on iron for vegetarians.)

From about eight or nine months onward, when your baby is eating more and may be beginning to take less milk, making sure you offer him something from each of the main food groups every day, along with his milk feedings, will provide him with a good range of nutrients. Don't worry if he chooses not to eat some of each—he will balance out his diet over the course of a few days, provided he is allowed to choose freely.

The Importance of Variety

The best way to provide a good range of nutrients for your baby is to offer a truly varied diet each week. Having a variety of foods will also provide different tastes and textures for him to learn to manage—and the more naturally colorful the food is, the better the range of vitamins and minerals it is likely to contain.

It's a good idea to have a look at your own diet to see if you are buying the same foods (however healthy) week after week. If you are, try some new foods—even changing the cuts of meat or the type of bread you normally buy can provide you with a different selection of nutrients. Swapping wheat-based meals for other grains, such as oats or rye, now and then will add extra vitamins and minerals, and varying the fruit and vegetables you buy, and including some fresh herbs, will also help to ensure a wide range of nutrients for the whole family. (Meal planning can help with this; see page 41.)

"Because Charlotte eats with us she has tasted and loves curry, chili, Japanese, Italian, Caribbean, and Thai foods—in fact the more flavor the better. The only three things she hates with a passion are banana, carrot, and cheese. We have no battles, and mealtimes are fun—eating out is brilliant."

—Samantha, mother of Charlotte, 1 year

Foods to Avoid

Although your baby can share most of the food you eat, you need to take care with some ingredients, which are bad for babies. These are discussed below, starting with the most important—salt.

Salt

A baby's immature kidneys can't cope with too much sodium, and it can make them very ill, so it's important to avoid it as much as possible. A high-sodium diet early on may also make babies more prone to high blood pressure later in life.

Salt shouldn't be added to any food that is going to be offered to your baby. If you are used to adding salt to your cooking at home, you'll probably find cooking with lemon, herbs, and spices can satisfy your need for a "fuller" flavor—or you can add salt to your own food at the table.

However, while it's relatively easy to avoid salt when you're cooking from scratch, most (around 80 percent) of the salt we eat is "hidden" in processed foods as a flavor enhancer and preservative, so it's important to know what to look out for when you are buying food. The worst culprits are ready-made gravies, stocks, soups and sauces, canned foods, and frozen meals.

Checking labels will help you to choose healthier options—some types and brands of bread, croissants, and pastries (especially those baked in-store or served in cafés and restaurants) contain much more salt than others that look the same. Even some bottled mineral waters have very high salt levels. Baked beans, cheese, and ham can vary enormously, too, depending on the brand. Once you've worked out which brand has the least salt you can just buy that one again next time, so you don't have to read the labels on every shopping trip.

However, labels can be confusing because manufacturers are required to list how much sodium the food contains, rather than how much salt. This can make a product appear less salty than it really is—to work out the salt content you need to multiply the sodium content by 2.5. Official advice in the United States is to minimize salt for babies. Guidelines in the UK are more specific (and recommended salt limits for adults are lower), so we have included them here as a useful reference.

Total daily salt (sodium) limits, as recommended by the UK Departments of Health

Child's age	Daily salt limit	Equivalent in sodium
6 to 12 months	1g	0.4g (400mg)
1 to 2 years	2g	0.8g (800mg)

Note: The UK's recommended daily limit for adults is 6g of salt—or 2.4g of sodium.

Food with more than 0.5g (500 mg) salt per 100g is classed as very salty, so your baby should have only the smallest amount, if any. Some foods have as much as 4g (400 mg) of salt per 100g—or even more. Even a small amount of one of these foods could exceed your baby's recommended daily salt limit. It's all too easy to give babies more salt than they should have, so it really is worth taking the time to check.

At a Glance—Salty Foods

The following foods are fairly salty, but they are okay for babies to have in small quantities occasionally. Try not to offer your baby more than one food from this list in any one day:

- Breakfast cereals with high salt/sugar levels (choose the lowest you can find)
- Hard cheeses, such as Cheddar, and processed varieties such as Edam
- Sausages, especially pepperoni, chorizo, and salami-type sausages
- Ham and bacon
- Smoked or salted fish, such as smoked salmon and anchovies
- Foods preserved in brine, such as tuna and olives (choose those preserved in oil or spring water instead)
- Baked beans (choose low-sodium and low-sugar varieties, preferably organic)
- Frozen or take-out pizza
- Store-bought baked goods such as focaccia, pastries, and cheese straws.

The following foods are very salty and are not suitable for babies:

- Potato chips, tortilla chips, and other salty snacks
- Ready-made potpies
- Many frozen food meals
- Most take-out foods and "fast foods," such as burgers, pizzas, etc.
- Some ready-made sauces for pasta and other dishes
- Most ready-made gravies and stocks, including granules and cubes (choose lower-salt versions)
- Sauces such as ketchup, barbecue sauce, and soy sauce
- Canned or packet (dried) soups
- Processed cheese foods, such as string cheese.

Balancing Salt

When you're planning meals, it's worth bearing in mind the amount of something salty your baby is likely to eat. A meal that consists only of ham, cheese, and salty bread could well put a strain on his kidneys, but one that includes a small amount of ham alongside plenty of vegetables and fruit is unlikely to cause him any harm. If you are eating at a restaurant or at a relative's house, where the food could contain a lot of salt, try to make sure that your child is offered the most nutritious parts of the meal with as little gravy or sauce as possible. If he does have something very salty, make sure he can drink as much water (or breast milk) as he needs, both with the meal and later, and that his other meals that day are low in salt.

"We really don't make anything different for Ed. At first we had to get used to eating food without salt, but now we are used to it there isn't anything I wouldn't offer him—I just don't think about it now. We have healthy food—he has what we have." —Ria, mother of Jake, 2 years, and Ed, 10 months

Other Foods to Avoid

There are several other foods that babies shouldn't be offered, besides salt. Some, such as raw shellfish or undercooked eggs, carry a risk of food poisoning or infection; some can cause harm such as tooth decay; while others simply don't contain enough nutrients.

Sugar

Sugar provides only "empty calories"—it doesn't have any essential nutrients. It also contributes to tooth decay. If you can avoid giving your child a sugary diet in the early years, he is less likely to crave very sweet things as he gets older. Children will only expect a sweet dessert at mealtimes if they usually have one (and if they do, they will quickly learn to save some room for their dessert by eating less of their main course). Some foods aimed at children, such as cereals or flavored yogurts, can contain a lot of sugar—every 5g of sugar mentioned on the label is about a teaspoonful of sugar. Sucrose, dextrose, fruit syrup, and glucose are all forms of sugar, too.

Sweet dishes that include a small amount of sugar are okay to offer your baby occasionally, especially if they're otherwise nutritious (homemade apple pie or fruit cake, for example). Ingredients such as dried or fresh fruits can often be used as a sweetener, with no need for any extra sugar at all. And adding sweet spices, such as cinnamon, to dessert and cake recipes helps to enhance their overall sweetness.

Don't be tempted to use an artificial sweetener to replace real sugar in your recipes, or to buy foods that are low in sugar but contain artificial sweeteners (such as aspartame)—they carry their own health risks, and they won't stop your child developing a liking for very sweet food.

Candies contain no useful nutrients and can fill babies' tummies, leaving little room for more nutritious foods. They are also likely to contain additives (see below).

Additives

Additives such as monosodium glutamate and artificial preservatives, flavors, and sweeteners, should be avoided as much as possible. Research has found a correlation between hyperactivity in children and the consumption of certain food colorings (often found in candies and desserts) together with the preservative sodium benzoate. The additives to watch out for are: Tartrazine, Sunset yellow, and Allura red (Yellow No. 5, Yellow No. 6, and Red No. 40). Three more, Quinoline yellow, Carmoisine, and Ponceau 4R (Yellow No. 10, Red No. 10, and Acid Red No. 18), are not allowed in food in the United States, but may be found in Canada.

Frozen Entrées and Junk Foods

Ready-meals such as frozen entrées—even those labeled as "low fat"—and junk foods, such as cheap burgers, pizzas, and pies, are completely unsuitable for babies. In general, these foods are very highly processed and contain a great deal of salt, sugar, artificial additives, and hydrogenated fats, with very few nutrients.

Honey

Babies shouldn't have honey until they are over one year old because it can be the source of an infection called botulism.

Certain Types of Fish

Shark, swordfish, and marlin should be avoided because they contain potentially high levels of mercury, which can affect the development of the nervous system. Raw shell-fish carry a high risk of food poisoning—they are safe only if thoroughly cooked. Although oily fish (such as salmon, trout, mackerel, herring, sardines, and fresh tuna) is very nutritious, girls and women of childbearing age shouldn't eat it more than twice a week because of the possible buildup of pollutants (boys, men, and older women can have up to four portions per week). Canned tuna doesn't contain the same toxins as fresh tuna or other oily fish, so it can be eaten more often.

Undercooked Eggs

Eggs often contain salmonella, which can make a baby very ill. Cooking destroys the bug, so provided they are thoroughly cooked so that the yolk is firm, eggs can form part of your baby's diet. (The old advice to avoid egg whites is not relevant for babies over six months, as babies this age are better able to tolerate them.) Foods that contain raw or undercooked eggs—including mayonnaise, desserts such as chocolate mousse or tiramisù, and some ice creams (particularly homemade)—shouldn't be given to babies.

Bran and High-Fiber Foods

Raw bran and high-fiber cereals (such as All-bran and some muesli) can interfere with the absorption of iron and other essential nutrients, so they are not good for babies. They are also very filling and don't contain enough calories or nutrients. If you are offering wholegrain cereals (such as brown rice and pasta) make sure your baby has a choice of some carbohydrate-rich foods that contain less fiber as well.

Hydrogenated Fats

Hydrogenated fats, also known as trans-fatty acids, are thought to interfere with the beneficial actions of healthy fats. Although many processed foods have eliminated them, they are still found in some store-bought cookies, pies, potato chips, frozen entrées, and in some margarines and lard. Most healthy foods don't contain them.

Drinks to Avoid

The only drinks babies really need with their solid meals are water and breast milk (which can be a thirst-quenching drink as well as a food). Other drinks will tend to fill your baby up, leaving no room for more nutritious food or milk feedings.

Caffeinated drinks, such as coffee, tea, and cola, can make babies irritable; tea also interferes with iron absorption. Fizzy or fruit-flavored drinks are very sugary and acidic (so not good for teeth) and many contain additives. Pure fruit juice is okay in small quantities, but it should be diluted one part juice to ten parts water.

Cows' milk shouldn't be given as a drink to babies under one year old because it fills them up with the wrong balance of nutrients. The same applies to goats' and sheep's milks. It's okay, though, to use these milks in cooking or—provided they are pasteurized—with breakfast cereals, for babies of six months and older.

Allergies

Although babies over six months are able to tolerate a wider range of foods than younger babies, if there is a history of food allergies in your family it's a good idea to introduce solid foods carefully. Allowing three days between foods that may be likely

Common allergens

Foods you may wish to introduce carefully if there are allergies in the family:

- Cows' milk (also goats' and sheep's milk)
- Eggs
- Peanuts (which aren't true nuts but are related to legumes)
- Wheat (and other grains that contain gluten)
- Soybeans
- Fish
- Shellfish
- Nuts
- Seeds (especially sesame)
- Citrus fruits
- Tomatoes
- Strawberries

to cause a problem will give you time to spot a reaction (such as itchy skin or a rash, diarrhea, vomiting, stomach pain, swollen lips, sore eyes, or wheezing). Breastfeeding for as long as possible will help to reduce the risk of allergies, and is especially protective while new foods are being introduced. It's also important to have a truly varied diet, so that your baby doesn't eat too much of any one food. If you suspect a food allergy or intolerance, talk to your doctor.

"Polly was spoon-fed and had allergies, and has always been a bit picky. But, now she sees her baby sister eating lots of new things, she'll try them. Evie is encouraging her to be more adventurous."
—Anisa, mother of Polly, 3 years, and Evie, 8 months

Vegetarian Diets

If you are planning to bring your baby up as a vegetarian you'll need to make sure he has plenty of iron and protein from nonmeat sources. Fish (if you eat it), eggs, tofu, and dried beans and legumes, such as lentils, chickpeas, and split peas, are good sources of both protein and iron. Dried fruit, such as apricots and figs, and (low-sugar, low-salt) fortified cereals can also be a useful source of iron. The absorption of iron is helped by vitamin C, so it's a good idea to include foods that are high in vitamin C, such as red berries, tomatoes and citrus fruits, with meals, or to offer diluted, freshly squeezed fruit juice as a drink.

Vegan diets are generally considered to be too low in important fats, B vitamins, zinc, calcium, and some amino acids (as well as iron) to be safe for babies and so supplements are almost always needed. Breastfeeding for at least two years, if possible, will help to ensure good nutrition, but we recommend you talk to a nutritionist or dietitian if you want your baby to have a vegan diet.

Chapter Five
MAKING MEALTIMES SIMPLE

Baby-led weaning is an easy way to feed your baby, but organizing family mealtimes can still be tricky for busy parents. Here are some ideas to make it a little easier.

Cooking with a Baby

Even if you are an experienced cook, preparing a meal when you have a baby or toddler can present new challenges—especially if you have gone back to work. Babies' patterns are unpredictable, and most babies will need some attention in less time than it takes to cook the average meal. So you will probably need to take advantage of small chunks of baby-free time whenever you can—and to find creative ways of doing things when you can't.

Some babies are quite happy to sit for short periods in a bouncy chair or to lie on a mat with their toys while their mom or dad cooks, provided they can see them. An older baby may be content to sit in her highchair with some snacks and watch you. A sling can be really useful—preferably one that you can wear on your back or side as well as your front, so that your baby can snuggle up to you safely, away from any hot pans, oven doors, and sharp knives. Most babies will settle in a sling for long periods of time, and may even fall asleep there.

Getting family meals on the table is easier if you can break down your cooking tasks into stages and work out what can be done when. For example, you may be able to make your pasta sauce ahead of time or wash and peel your vegetables and put them in the fridge early in the day to be cut up later for an evening meal.

"Arthur loves to watch me cook. He'll sit in his highchair with a rice cake and I'll talk about all the food as I'm preparing it and show him what I'm doing—he's quite happy." —Caroline, mother of Arthur, 11 months

Batch Cooking and Freezing

Cooking in bulk—or batch cooking—is a great way to save time (and money) and is invaluable when you are especially busy or if you return to work after maternity leave. Many dishes and sauces can be frozen successfully, enabling you to thaw out either a complete meal or one that's already half-made.

Some parents buy in bulk and spend a couple of hours cooking large amounts and freezing it in smaller portions. Others simply cook twice as much as they need when they're making something like lasagna, and freeze half. Even preparing and freezing small portions of things such as chopped onions or grated cheese can make a difference.

Foods Suitable for Preparing In Advance

- Main dishes, such as lasagna, meatballs, burgers, chili, stew, and meatloaf
- Stocks, soups, and sauces, including pasta sauces and homemade gravy
- Cooked ground meat with onions (to use for dishes such as shepherd's pie)
- Preprepared vegetables (especially anything difficult to chop with a baby on your hip, such as onions), fruit, and grated cheese
- Uncooked dough, and batter for bread, some cakes, muffins, scones, and pancakes
- Spare ingredients, such as tomato paste and lemon juice (freeze in ice cube trays).

Tips for Freezing Home-Cooked Food

- Cooked food should be allowed to cool at room temperature, then transferred into suitable airtight containers and frozen as soon as possible.
- Dividing food into small or individual portions before freezing helps it to freeze (and defrost) more quickly. (Sauce can be divided into portions in a muffin tin [or yogurt containers]; once frozen, put them into a single container for storage.)
- Food expands when frozen, so containers should be left around a third empty.
- It can be hard to identify frozen food, so remember to label containers with the contents and date.
- Freezers should be set at 0°F or below. If you are planning to freeze a lot of food in one go, set your freezer temperature to –9°F at least 24 hours beforehand.
- The maximum storage time for most frozen home-cooked food is around two to three months (to retain nutrients, taste and appearance).
- The majority of food is best defrosted slowly in the fridge before it is reheated. If you defrost food in a microwave, reheat it straight away.
- Defrosted meals should be eaten within 24 hours of removing from the freezer.
- Defrosted foods should be reheated thoroughly. Check that the food is steaming hot in the middle before serving (but let it cool before offering it to your baby).
- Any leftovers should be thrown away—don't refreeze or reheat anything twice.

Meal Planning

Planning ahead can make organizing mealtimes, food shopping—and batch cooking—much easier. It's also a useful way to make sure you are offering your baby a variety of tastes and textures. Many families get into a pattern of eating the same few favorite dishes each week without really realizing it—planning can help you avoid this.

Writing down an outline of your main meals for a two-week period will help you to see at a glance whether there's a good balance of main ingredients, and to spot "same-old" meals. If you notice any foods, textures, or tastes that are missing, you can choose some new recipes or ingredients to fill the gaps.

Food Safety

Kitchens can be a breeding ground for the bacteria that cause food poisoning, so it's important to follow some basic rules to keep you and your family safe.

Routine Food Hygiene

Wash your hands thoroughly with soap and warm water and dry them before handling food, between the handling of raw and ready-to-eat foods, after touching the trash can, after handling cleaning materials, after changing your baby's diaper and after touching pets, their bedding, or food bowls. Everyone in the family should wash their hands before eating (wash your baby's hands before offering him food).

Kitchen surfaces should be cleaned before and after you prepare food. Chopping boards and knives should always be washed thoroughly after use, but you need to be extra careful after cutting up raw meat or fish. Having a separate chopping board for raw fish and meat will help to prevent the spread of harmful bacteria.

Storing and Cooking Food

Perishable food should be kept in the fridge, which should be set between 34 and 41°F. Adding warm foods or leaving the door open will raise the temperature, so make sure food has cooled down fully before putting it in the fridge and try not to open the door more than necessary. Raw meat and fish should be covered, on a plate or in a bag (especially when defrosting), and kept on the lowest shelf, to prevent any juices from touching or dripping onto other foods. Highly perishable foods should be stored on the shelves rather than in the fridge door (which is the least cold part of the fridge).

Always cook food thoroughly, paying attention to cooking times and temperatures given in recipes. Take care with foods that need special preparation, such as some dried beans (see page 45), and consider buying fridge and meat thermometers.

Leftovers should be cooled, then put into the fridge as soon as possible, especially any dishes that contain meat, chicken, fish, seafood, eggs, or rice. Rice that is not to be eaten right away should be cooled, by washing it with cold water, then refrigerated immediately. This is because the spores of some food-poisoning bugs multiply in rice (and other grains) at room temperature and cannot be killed, even if the food is thoroughly reheated. All cooked foods and leftovers should be kept at the top of the fridge and eaten within two days.

Finally, follow storage instructions given on food packages, check "best before" dates regularly, and don't give your baby foods that are past their "use by" date.

Part Two
The Recipes

These recipes are all baby-led weaning favorites. They are easy to make, tasty, and nutritious, and will provide a range of tastes and textures for your baby to explore and for everyone to enjoy. Don't be afraid to experiment with the recipes—they are not set in stone. Most of them are fairly simple, and the ingredients or amounts (or even methods) can often be changed or adapted. We've made some suggestions, but really it's up to you. Enjoy!

Getting Started

Some Notes on Ingredients

- Try to use **fresh ingredients** as far as possible, and, when you can, go for produce that is seasonal, locally grown, and organic. The flavor of these foods is often better, and with organic foods you can guarantee that your baby won't be exposed to the chemicals commonly used in food production.
- Where a recipe includes **milk**, this means whole cow's milk, unless otherwise stated. Most of the recipes should also work with other animal milks or with rice or soy milks, but we can't guarantee this.
- **Flour** is assumed to be wheat flour, also called all-purpose flour, unless otherwise stated. Generally, it is considered safe for babies over six months to eat wheat, but it may be an ingredient you prefer to avoid if you have intolerances in the family (see page 37). Spelt flour is made from a type of wheat that is easier to digest than ordinary wheat. Or you may prefer to use a gluten-free flour, such as buckwheat (not wheat, despite the name), rice, corn, or potato flour. Gluten-free flours are generally okay for cooking, although they may result in a slightly different texture and won't work in recipes that use yeast.
- Aim to use unsalted **butter** wherever possible, because it's better for babies than butter containing salt. If you would rather not use dairy products, you can use oil, or a vegetable-based margarine (one that is free from hydrogenated oils or trans-fats).
- When the recipe refers simply to **cheese**, you can use any hard cheese, such as Cheddar, Monterey Jack, Swiss, or Emmental. These will all work in recipes where the cheese is grated and needs to melt. Nonmelting cheeses, such as halloumi, feta, and ricotta, won't work in these recipes.
- Where a recipe calls for **cream cheese**, this means a white cream cheese, such as Philadelphia (or alternatively, in some recipes, mascarpone).
- The weights in the recipes are for dried **pasta and noodles**, rather than fresh (which weigh more). Most pasta is wheat-based and fresh pasta usually contains egg, so if you are trying to avoid these foods you will need to use an alternative, such as rice noodles or corn pasta.
- Dried **herbs** are more concentrated than fresh; as a general rule 1 teaspoon of dried herbs is equivalent to 3 teaspoons (1 tablespoon) of fresh herbs. (To chop fresh herbs easily, use a pair of sharp scissors, and chop over a bowl or in a cup.)

- **Ginger** means root ginger.
- For **lemon, lime, or orange zest**, use a fine grater to take off the extreme outside, or colored part, of the rind of the fruit—the whitish pith can be very bitter.
- Where a recipe calls for **breadcrumbs**—unless it says fresh—it means stale or dried. To make breadcrumbs, grate day-old bread (dry it in the oven first if necessary).
- Fresh and dried **chilies** (flakes and powder) vary in potency so start by using a little until you find out how hot your baby likes his food. The "heat" from raw chili pepper can linger for hours, so be careful not to touch your baby's hands, eyes, nose or mouth or to change his diaper before you've washed your hands thoroughly.
- Where a recipe uses canned **beans and legumes** (for example, chickpeas or red kidney beans), dried versions can be used instead but may need presoaking and/or precooking (see chart below). Although you can use different types of beans in most dishes, you may need to adjust the recipe preparation time. Take care if using red kidney beans or soybeans—they can be harmful if they are not soaked and cooked for long enough (canned varieties are ready to eat). Lentils, split peas, black-eyed peas and mung beans don't need any presoaking or precooking.

Soaking and cooking times for beans and legumes

	Presoaking time	Precooking time	Cooking time to soften
Chickpeas, cranberry beans, butter beans, cannellini beans, black beans, fava beans, flageolet beans, lima beans, pinto beans, azuki beans	Up to 12 hours	No precooking needed, but boiling them for 10 minutes will cut down the cooking time	Up to 1 hour
Red kidney beans	Up to 12 hours	10 minutes, boiling rapidly	45 to 60 minutes
Soybeans	Up to 12 hours	1 hour, boiling rapidly	2 to 3 hours

To presoak: Put the dried beans into a large pan or bowl, pour in cold water equivalent to triple volume, cover and leave for the required time. Drain and rinse.

To precook: Put the presoaked beans into a pan of fresh water, bring them to a boil and boil rapidly (not simmering) for the required time. Drain and rinse.

Technical Stuff

Ovens

The recipes give instructions for cooking using a standard oven, although some recipes include an alternative method for microwaves. However, if you want to use a microwave for part of a recipe, such as precooking vegetables or melting butter, that's fine.

Most ovens take at least 15 minutes to heat, and it's usually best to wait until the oven is at the required temperature before putting the food in. Broilers also need to be preheated.

Unless they are a convection oven, all ovens tend to be hotter at the top, affecting how fast food cooks (and whether or not it gets burned!); you can cook two dishes that require slightly different temperatures in the oven at the same time by putting them on different racks.

Temperatures given in recipes are always a guide only, so you will need to experiment with your own oven to get a feel for whether you need to adjust the temperatures up or down. If you have a convection oven you may find that the food cooks better at slightly lower temperatures than those given in most recipes so you will need to adjust your timings accordingly.

Basic Cooking Terms

- To **sift** flour pass it through a fine sieve, shaking gently. This adds air and removes lumps. If using whole-grain flour, add the bran left in the sieve to the sifted flour.
- To **simmer** a dish in a pan, the liquid should be just bubbling occasionally; when **boiling**, the liquid should be bubbling continuously.
- **Parboiling** means boiling for part of the time needed to fully cook the food.
- **Blanching** means putting food very briefly into boiling water. (This is all the cooking needed for some vegetables—spinach for example.) Some recipes suggest blanching tomatoes to loosen the skin so they can be peeled more easily.
- **Sautéing** is frying food quickly in hot oil in a shallow pan.

BREAKFAST

Don't be surprised if your baby shows no interest in breakfast for the first few months of solid foods; all many babies want first thing in the morning is hugging and a milk feeding. Once your baby is ready to join in with breakfast, however, there are plenty of ways you can adapt your usual food or try something new.

It's easy for adults to get into a habit of having the same thing for breakfast every day, but it's a good idea to vary what you offer to your baby so that he has the chance to discover different tastes and textures and get a good range of nutrients.

The recipes that follow will give you some ideas for tasty alternatives to your "usual" breakfast—and many of them will work just as well for lunch, too.

Breakfast Ideas

Here are some tips for really simple breakfasts for your baby.

Fresh Fruit

Fresh fruit, served whole or sliced (see page 19) makes a superb breakfast.

Fruit with Yogurt

A note on cereals: *Many breakfast cereals aren't really suitable for babies; those aimed at children are often very salty and/or sugary, and some that are good for adults (high-fiber, bran-based cereals) are not good for babies.*

Fresh, stewed or puréed fruit, served with full-fat natural yogurt (preferably with active live cultures) is a simple but delicious breakfast. Your toddler can stir the fruit in while your baby can practice dipping skills or using a spoon, either preloaded by you and offered to him or, when he can manage it, loaded himself.

Super-Cooked Egg

An overcooked fried or poached egg is solid enough for a baby to pick up easily and is a good way to help him discover the difference between the white and the yolk. Just fry or poach an egg as normal (using the minimum of oil if frying), but leave it cooking until the yolk is firm all the way through. Let it cool a bit, then trim off any crispy edges.

French Toast

French toast makes a great breakfast—or your baby may enjoy it cold as a snack.

Serves 1 adult and 1 baby

2 eggs

A little milk (optional—it makes the eggs go further)

4 slices of bread

Oil or butter (preferably unsalted) for frying

In a bowl, beat the eggs and add the milk, if using. Dip the bread into the egg mix, turning as necessary to coat both sides.

Heat the oil or butter in a frying pan and fry the soaked bread on both sides over medium to high heat until the egg is thoroughly cooked and the whole thing is golden brown.

Cut into pieces (finger shapes are usually easiest for young babies; toddlers may prefer triangles) and serve immediately, or once cool enough for your baby to handle.

Storage: *French toast is best eaten fresh, but can be frozen and reheated in a microwave. To freeze, allow to cool completely and pack in an airtight container, separating the slices with wax or parchment paper.*

Option

• Add a pinch of cinnamon to the beaten egg mix for a warm, spicy flavor.

Scrambled Eggs

Scrambled eggs make a healthy start to your day—just check that your baby's portion is cooked through before offering it.

Serves 1 adult and 1 baby

3 eggs
1 tablespoon milk (optional—it gives a softer consistency)
Pinch of freshly ground black pepper (optional)
Small pat of butter (preferably unsalted)

In a bowl, beat the eggs then add the milk (if using) and black pepper to taste.

Melt the butter in a nonstick frying pan over a gentle heat. Pour in the egg mixture and keep stirring as it thickens. Continue for 5 to 10 minutes until all the egg has set. (You can also cook scrambled eggs in a bowl in the microwave. Use the HIGH setting and cook for about 1 minute, stirring and checking every 15 seconds.)

Serve immediately, or once cool enough for your baby, with toast, a bagel, an English muffin, or a croissant.

Options

- You can add anything you like to the egg mixture provided it will cook (or heat through) in the time it takes the egg to cook. Try a little finely chopped ham, cooked sausage or salami; some grated cheese; a few thinly sliced mushrooms (canned or precooked); or some finely chopped onion (this is best softened first by frying gently in the butter before the egg mixture goes in).
- Adding some herbs, such as finely chopped fresh parsley, to the egg mixture or sprinkling paprika on top of the cooked egg will give it extra flavor.

Extra-Thick Oatmeal

Oatmeal is a really healthy breakfast for all the family but it can be tricky for babies to manage. This extra-thick version can be picked up in handfuls. (Your baby will also enjoy squeezing and smearing it, so a long-sleeved bib or bare arms will help with cleanup.)

Serves 1 baby

3 level tablespoons quick-cooking oats (not "instant" oats; use old-fashioned rolled oats for a chunkier texture)

½ cup water or milk, or a mixture of the two (according to your taste)

Put the oats into a small saucepan and add the water or milk. Bring to a boil and simmer for 5 to 6 minutes, stirring continuously. Allow to "sit" off the heat for a few minutes, then serve warm. (You can also make oatmeal in a bowl in the microwave. Use the HIGH setting and cook for about 2 minutes, stirring and checking every 30 to 60 seconds.)

Option

• Fruit is ideal for adding to oatmeal. However, if it is cooked with the oatmeal it usually stays hot for longer, so check the temperature of the fruit as well as the oatmeal before offering it to your baby. Try adding some grated apple or pear (with or without a pinch of cinnamon) during the cooking; a few fresh blueberries, or any stewed or puréed fruit (apricot, prunes, plums, apple, pear, etc.) during the cooking or stirred in afterward; a little molasses drizzled on top after cooking (this will make the oatmeal messier—but it does have lots of healthy B vitamins!).

Note: If you want thinner oatmeal, just use more milk (or a mixture of milk and water).

"Stewed plums, cooked with a cinnamon stick, has been a real winner. It's really good to freeze in ice cubes and add to oatmeal in the morning."
—Jane, mother of Mia, 7 months

Quick Oatmeal Fingers

These little fingers are a very easy way for a baby just starting out to manage oats—although adults will probably want to stick to "real" oatmeal. This recipe takes just a couple of minutes in the microwave, so it's great if you're in a hurry.

"Nils used to love quick oatmeal fingers—they seemed so plain to me but he could get hold of them and get quite a lot in, which he seemed to need at breakfast once he got to eight months or so. And I loved them because there was no mess first thing in the morning!" —Kate, mother of Nils, 2½ years

Serves 1 adult and 1 baby

3 level tablespoons quick-cooking oats (not "instant" oats)
3 tablespoons milk

In a bowl, soak the oats in the milk until you have a mushy mixture.

Press the mixture into a small, flat-bottomed microwave-safe dish or bowl using the back of a spoon. Cook in the microwave for 2 minutes on HIGH.

Cut into fingers while still hot and serve when cool.

Options

• Try pressing some ready-to-eat raisins or dried cranberries into the top of the oat mixture before you cook it.
• If you don't have a microwave, you can also make oatmeal fingers in the oven. Simply cook for about 15 minutes at 375°F.

Drop Scones (Scotch Pancakes)

Drop scones are pancakes made with a slightly thicker version of Classic Pancake batter (see opposite). They can be served for breakfast or, with added fillings, for lunch. Like all pancakes, they work best when the pan gets really hot—so don't be surprised if the first one isn't quite as good as the rest.

Makes up to 20 drop scones

1 cup all-purpose flour
1 teaspoon baking powder
1 egg
⅔ cup milk, plus more if necessary
Oil (or butter, preferably unsalted) for frying

Stir the flour and baking powder together in a mixing bowl, make a well in the center, and break the egg into it. Pour in half the milk, then beat or whisk the ingredients together, starting in the middle and gradually working in the flour. Slowly add the remaining milk and continue beating until any lumps have disappeared and the consistency is like heavy cream, adding more milk if needed. Stir in any additional ingredients (see options, below).

Heat a flat griddle or large nonstick frying pan with a very thin coating of oil. When the pan is really hot, pour in small amounts of batter—about 2 tablespoons each time—so it spreads to 3 to 4 inches. Cook for a few minutes, until the edges are cooked and the top is set almost to the middle, then flip over the drop scone and cook it for the same length of time on the other side. If you have a big pan you can cook several drop scones at once.

Serve warm or cold, plain, or with a savory or sweet spread.

> **Storage:** *Drop scones can be frozen; freeze them in an airtight container, separated with sheets of wax paper so they don't stick together. They keep for a couple of months and can be reheated in seconds under a broiler or in the microwave.*

Option

• You can add a little of anything you fancy to the mixture before cooking (take care though—too much will change the consistency). Try a little grated cheese (Cheddar or similar); some chopped spinach; some finely chopped red bell pepper; a few raisins; a few blueberries, squashed or cut in half; a little grated apple; or a little mashed banana.

Classic Pancakes

Pancakes are the classic weekend breakfast, and once you've made them a few times you'll find them very quick and easy. Thin pancakes can be rolled up and then cut into pinwheels to make them more grabbable for babies. For thicker pancakes, just reduce the amount of milk (or milk and water). Experiment with the consistency to get your perfect pancake.

Makes about 15 pancakes

1 cup all-purpose flour

1 egg

1½ cups milk (or half water and half milk for thinner pancakes)

Oil or butter (preferably unsalted) for frying

Tip: *Pancake batter can be used for Yorkshire puddings (see page 99) and Toad-in-the-Hole (see page 96); it will keep for a few days in the fridge. Cooked pancakes can be frozen (separated with sheets of parchment or wax paper) for up to two months.*

To make the batter, put the flour into a mixing bowl, make a well in the center, and break the egg into it. Pour in half the milk (or milk and water), and beat or whisk the ingredients together, starting in the middle and gradually working in the flour. Gradually add the rest of the liquid and continue beating until any lumps have disappeared and the consistency is like heavy cream. If you have time, leave the batter to rest for an hour or two in the fridge before cooking.

Next, heat a flat griddle or large frying pan with a very thin coating of oil or butter. When the pan is really hot, pour in a ladleful of batter and tilt the pan so it spreads out evenly and thinly. Allow to cook for about 3 minutes until bubbles are bursting over the whole surface. Gently lift around the edge to check that the underside is golden. At this point you should be able to jiggle the pan so that the whole pancake is loose. Flip the pancake over (toss it if you can!) and continue cooking for about 30 seconds.

Serve warm, either with a topping (see below) or a sauce. The simplest sauce is a squeeze of lemon juice or some plain yogurt.

Options

• For a richer batter, add 1 to 2 teaspoons of oil or melted butter.
• Try spreading one of the following on your pancake before folding or rolling it up: ham or spinach with grated cheese for a savory option; cream cheese; mashed banana; grated apple with raisins and cinnamon; or a few squashed blueberries or raspberries.

On Toast ...

You can put pretty much anything on a piece of toast at breakfast time, but if you always go for jam or jelly here are some healthier alternatives to offer your baby. Fingers of toast are probably the easiest shape to start off with—older babies and toddlers may prefer small triangles. Try some of the following toppings:

- Hummus (see page 67)
- Cheese, such as cottage cheese or cream cheese
- Banana, mashed or sliced
- Sardines, in oil rather than brine (see page 61)
- Canned tuna or salmon
- Tomatoes, mashed or sliced
- Bean spread (see page 69)
- Baked beans, low-sugar and low-sodium
- Or even those portions of puréed vegetables that you made and froze before you heard of baby-led weaning!

Toast alternatives:
- White, wheat, or other whole-grain bread— whichever you don't normally have (see page 157)
- Rye bread
- Fruit bread (see page 159)
- Pita bread
- Chapatis (see page 161)
- Bagels, low-salt
- English muffins, split in half (see page 163)
- Drop scones (see page 52)
- Croissants, low-salt
- Rice cakes, low-salt

Tip: *Toasting the bread on one side only (under the broiler rather than in a toaster) and putting spread on the untoasted side will help it to stick better and make the slice softer.*

Light Lunches

L ight meals are ideal for you and your baby at lunchtime or even at supper, and this section has lots of ideas for meals that won't take too long to prepare and won't leave you feeling too full.

Cheese and Lentil Wedges

These tasty wedges are great for picnics or as a snack.

Serves 2 adults and 1 baby, generously

1 cup red lentils, rinsed thoroughly in cold water and drained
2 cups water
Oil or butter (preferably unsalted) for frying
1 large onion, finely chopped
¾ cup (3 to 4 ounces) grated cheese
1 teaspoon dried mixed herbs
1 egg, beaten
½ cup fresh breadcrumbs
Freshly ground black pepper, to taste

Put the lentils into a pan with the water. Bring to a boil, then cover and simmer for 10 to 15 minutes until the lentils are soft and all the liquid is absorbed. Check occasionally and skim off any froth. Meanwhile, heat the oil or butter in a frying pan, add the onion, and fry until soft.

Preheat the oven to 375°F and lightly grease a 9-inch cake pan. Drain the lentils and the onion and put them into a mixing bowl. Add the other ingredients and mix well. Press into the prepared pan using the back of a spoon.

Bake for about 30 minutes. Allow to cool slightly, then cut into wedges. Serve warm or cold.

Bubble and Squeak

This traditional British dish is great for babies once they are able to pick up handfuls of food and push it into their mouth. It's also a great way to use up leftover vegetables.

Serves 2 adults and 1 baby

1 pound potatoes, cooked and mashed—leftovers work best

8 ounces cooked cabbage, chopped

Pinch of freshly ground black pepper (optional)

½ teaspoon dried mixed herbs, or fresh equivalent (optional)

Oil or butter (preferably unsalted) for frying

Put the mashed potato, cabbage, pepper and herbs into a bowl and mix well.

Heat the oil or butter in a frying pan, add the potato mixture to cover the base of the pan and flatten it so it's about ½ to ¾ inch deep. Cook until the mixture is browned on the bottom, then turn it over and cook the other side, so it's browned on both sides and the middle is heated through. If you have a small pan you will need to cook the mixture in batches, adding a little more oil to the pan and preheating it each time. Alternatively, you can make individual patties of bubble and squeak by cooking small amounts separately.

Serve warm on its own, or it goes very well with baked beans, or as a side dish with cold chicken or turkey.

Options

- Although eggs don't appear in traditional bubble and squeak recipes, adding a beaten egg to the mixture will help bind it together and make it easier for your baby to hold.
- Adding half an onion or 2 scallions, finely chopped, then softened by frying gently in a little oil, will give some extra flavor.
- You can swap the cabbage for any precooked, chopped, or mashed vegetable (or combination of vegetables), for example: Brussels sprouts, kale, carrots, rutabagas, parsnips, celery, butternut squash, or zucchini.

Chickpea Patties

Chickpeas are very nutritious, and these patties, which are similar in flavor to falafel, are easy for a baby to hold and soft to eat. Making them with a blender or food processor is quickest, although you can also use a potato masher and wooden spoon.

Serves 2 adults and 1 baby

**One 15-ounce can chickpeas (or approx. ½ cup dried
    chickpeas, precooked—see page 45)**
**3 garlic cloves, finely chopped or crushed (unless you are
    using a blender)**
1 to 2 teaspoons ground coriander
1 to 2 teaspoons ground cumin
1 medium onion, chopped
Juice of ½ lemon (approx. 2 tablespoons)
1 tablespoon all-purpose flour
Approx. 2 tablespoons chopped fresh parsley
Freshly ground black pepper, to taste
Oil for frying

Rinse the chickpeas and drain them thoroughly. Combine them with the garlic, ground spices, onion, and lemon juice in a large bowl and mash them thoroughly with a potato masher (or use a blender or food processor). Add the flour, parsley, and black pepper and mix well.

Squeeze handfuls of the mixture into about 12 small patties (flouring or wetting your hands first will help to keep it from sticking). Put them in the fridge for about 20 minutes to firm up.

Heat the oil in a frying pan until it is very hot, then add the patties and fry for a few minutes on each side until crisp.

Chickpea patties are best served warm, inside warmed pita pockets, or with strips of pita bread with hummus (see page 67), tahini, Yogurt and Cucumber Dip (see page 68), or Spicy Tomato Salsa (see page 148).

Option

• If you want spicier patties, you can add a pinch of chili powder or some finely chopped chili pepper to the mixture.

Easy Dahl

This Indian dish is a mild introduction to spicy food and has plenty of healthy nutrients. It makes a good dip but it can also be eaten with a spoon or picked up in handfuls. If your baby is just starting out, offer her some ready-loaded dippers.

Serves 2 adults and 1 baby

Oil or butter (preferably unsalted) for frying

1 or 2 medium onions, chopped

2 garlic cloves, finely chopped or crushed

½ teaspoon turmeric

½ teaspoon ground cumin

½ teaspoon mild chili powder or chili flakes, to taste

½- to ¾-inch piece of fresh ginger, peeled and finely chopped or grated (optional)

1 cup yellow or red lentils, rinsed thoroughly in cold water and drained

1 cinnamon stick or ½ teaspoon ground cinnamon (optional)

Approx. 3⅓ cups water

Juice of ½ lemon (approx. 2 tablespoons) (optional)

1 tablespoon chopped fresh cilantro

Heat the oil or butter in a saucepan, add the onion, and fry until soft. Add the garlic and fry for another minute or two, then stir in the powdered spices and the ginger (if using). Add the lentils and cinnamon (if using), with enough water to cover them. Bring to a boil, stirring occasionally, then turn down the heat, cover, and simmer for 25 to 30 minutes, continuing to stir occasionally until the lentils are soft but not mushy.

Remove the cinnamon stick (if using), add the lemon juice and stir well. Sprinkle with the chopped cilantro and serve warm with other curries, Yogurt and Cucumber Dip (see page 68) and rice, naan bread, or chapatis (see page 161). Alternatively, use as a dip with strips of pita or chapati or sticks of vegetables.

Option

• You can also make dahl with yellow split peas, although these take longer to cook.

Tuna Croquettes

These little croquettes are delicious and really easy for babies to handle; they can also be made with salmon.

Serves 2 adults and 1 baby, generously

2 large potatoes

One 5-ounce can low-sodium tuna (in oil or spring water)

Juice of 1 lime (approx. 1 tablespoon), or to taste

2 tablespoons butter (preferably unsalted)

½ cup to 1 cup breadcrumbs (preferably dry or toasted)

Storage: *Cooked tuna croquettes keep for a couple of days in the fridge or they can be frozen. They can be reheated in a micro-wave or in the oven.*

Peel the potatoes and cut into small pieces and steam or boil them.

Preheat the oven to 400°F and lightly grease a large baking sheet. Drain the tuna and break it up.

When the potatoes are cooked, drain and mash them and add the tuna. Add the lime juice and mix well. Stir in the butter.

Shape the mixture into small sausages (flouring or wetting your hands will help to keep it from sticking), then roll each one in the breadcrumbs and put on the baking sheet. Bake in the oven for about 20 minutes, until browned and cooked through.

Serve warm, with vegetables, such as green beans and corn.

Pesto Pita Pockets

This simple recipe is just right for babies who can deal with chewier textures.

Pita bread pockets
1 teaspoon pesto sauce (low-sodium or homemade—see page 178) per pocket
2 tablespoons to ¼ cup grated cheese per pocket

Tip: Toasting the pita pockets lightly in a toaster first can make them easier to open.

Preheat the broiler. Open up the pita pockets and spread the pesto on the inside surfaces. Scatter the cheese on top of the pesto. Close the pockets and broil or microwave them for a few minutes, until the cheese has melted.

Cut into fingers (for your baby) while still hot and serve warm.

Pizza Toast

This is a cross between cheese on toast and a pizza; cut into fingers it's very easy for even beginner BLW babies to eat. The topping is great for wraps, too.

1 slice of bread (or more) per person
1 teaspoon tomato paste (low-sodium) per toast
¼ cup grated cheese, per toast
Sprinkling of dried oregano (or mixed herbs) per toast

Preheat the broiler. Toast (or broil) the bread on one side only. With the untoasted side up, spread the tomato paste on the bread and scatter the cheese and oregano evenly on top. Cook under the broiler until the cheese has melted.

Cut into fingers or triangles (for your baby) while still hot and serve warm.

Options

- Add your favorite toppings—chopped ham, mushrooms, roasted bell peppers, fresh tomatoes, etc.—just as you would with a traditional pizza.
- You can use a split English muffin instead of toast. For a crispy base, bake the muffin pizzas in the oven at 325°F for 10 to 15 minutes, rather than broiling.

Sardines on Toast

This is a simple, healthy lunch, made with plain canned sardines in oil (rather than the ones that come in a tomato or mustard sauce, which are usually quite salty).

Serves 2 adults and 1 baby

One 4-ounce can sardines (in olive oil)
6 to 8 ripe cherry tomatoes, roughly chopped
6 to 8 fresh basil leaves, chopped (to taste)
Bread for toasting (preferably rye or whole-grain)
Juice of ½ lemon (approx. 2 tablespoons) (optional)

Preheat the broiler. Drain the sardines and mash them (including the soft bones) with a fork. Add the tomatoes and mix well. Add the basil and stir well.

Put the bread under the broiler and toast it on one side only. Spread the sardine mixture on the untoasted side, then put it back under the broiler until warmed through.

Add a squeeze of lemon juice, if you like. Cut into fingers or triangles while still hot and serve warm with salad or Spicy Tomato Salsa (see page 148).

Arancini

Arancini are a delicious, easy finger food made from fresh or leftover risotto (see pages 136–139). They are traditionally filled with ham or mozzarella cheese. True arancini are little balls, but you can make unfilled ones stick-shaped if you prefer. To save leftover risotto so you can make arancini the next day, spread it in a shallow dish immediately after cooking so it cools as quickly as possible. When it's completely cool, transfer the risotto to an airtight container and put it in the fridge.

If you are making risotto just so you can make arancini, it's probably best to keep the recipe fairly simple—maybe just onion, garlic, and Parmesan cheese, together with the rice. Allow the cooked risotto to cool before you start to handle it.

Arancini sticks (and balls cut in half) make great dippers.

Serves 2 adults and 1 baby

A little flour for coating

1 egg, beaten

1 cup breadcrumbs, preferably stale or dried

2 cups cooked risotto, with any large chunks of other ingredients (such as chicken or carrots) removed

Some small pieces of mozzarella or ham (optional)

2 tablespoons oil for frying

Put the flour, egg, and breadcrumbs into three separate bowls. With wet hands, take about 1 tablespoon of risotto in the palm of your hand. Squash and mold it into a ball about the size of a golf ball, an oval or a short stick shape.

If you are filling the arancini, mold a ball and then make a hole in it with your finger. Gently push in a small piece of mozzarella and/or a small piece of ham, then press around the filling to cover it completely with the rice.

Dip each shape in flour, then into the beaten egg, and then into the breadcrumbs, so that it is coated thoroughly.

Heat the oil in a large frying pan, and when hot, add the arancini and cook for 5 to 10 minutes, turning them occasionally, until they're golden and crisp.

Serve warm. If you have filled the arancini with mozzarella, cut the balls in half before offering them to your baby and check that the cheese is not too hot.

Onigiri (Japanese Rice Balls)

Onigiri are very popular in Japan and are often put into lunchboxes or taken on picnics. They can be made plain or with a filling, such as grilled salmon, and wrapped in a strip of nori (edible seaweed) to add a different flavor and texture. Traditionally round or triangular, they can be made into any shape or size to suit your baby.

Sushi rice is the best rice for making onigiri, but you can use sticky rice or risotto rice instead. You can buy nori in any Japanese or Chinese market and in many major supermarkets.

Serves 2 adults and 1 baby

¾ cup Japanese sushi rice
Filling of your choice, in small pieces (e.g. salmon, avocado, canned tuna)
1 to 2 sheets of nori, cut into strips (optional)

Cook the rice according to the instructions on the package and allow to cool slightly.

With wet hands, take 1 to 2 tablespoons of warm rice and press into your cupped hand (or a small bowl), making a dent in the middle. Put in your chosen filling and mold the rice around it, pressing firmly and ensuring that the filling is completely covered.

Make the onigiri into a ball, sausage shape or triangle, to suit your baby, applying enough force, and adding a little warm water if needed, to stick the grains together firmly (or it will crumble). If you want, you can then wrap the onigiri with a strip of nori.

Serve warm or cold, on their own or with a dip.

Option

- Adults may like their onigiri filled with pickled plum, which is very salty and so not suitable for babies and young children.

Baked Potatoes

Baked potatoes are an excellent standby for lunch. They are best cooked slowly, in the oven, but they can also be cooked in about 10 minutes in a microwave.

> **1 large baking potato per person (the person with the biggest one gets to share with the baby)**
> **1 small pat of butter (preferably unsalted) per potato (optional)**
> **Topping of your choice (see below)**

Preheat the oven to 400°F. Choose potatoes of roughly similar sizes, scrub them thoroughly, dry them, and prick them all over with a fork. Put them in the oven (they don't need a baking sheet) and bake for about 1 hour, depending on their size (when done, they should feel soft when squeezed).

Baked potatoes are best served warm, with a pat of butter or a topping, and a side salad. Cut the potato into wedges for your baby, or split it wide open and let him help himself to soft handfuls of potato and topping. Alternatively, scoop out the inside of the potato, mix with the topping, then pile it all back into the skin.

Options

- Brushing the potatoes with oil before putting them in the oven makes the skins shiny and less dry.
- Sweet potatoes can also be baked (for slightly less time), but they tend to drip, so put them on a baking sheet.
- Ideas for toppings: grated cheese or cream cheese; baked beans; tuna with corn; mackerel with tomatoes; chili; Bolognese sauce; cooked beets with feta cheese.

> **Tip:** *Pushing a metal skewer through each potato (and leaving it in place) before putting them in the oven will reduce the cooking time.*

Healthy Chicken Nuggets

These are a lovely alternative to store-bought chicken nuggets—much healthier! They can be served with vegetables, as a main meal, or as a starter or snack. They're great for dipping too—try them with Homemade Tomato Ketchup (page 147).

Serves 2 adults and 1 baby

2 or 3 chicken breasts (or thigh-meat fillets)
1 egg
2 ounces breadcrumbs
1 teaspoon dried mixed herbs (optional)
Freshly ground black pepper, to taste
Oil or butter (preferably unsalted) for frying

Cut the chicken into finger shapes, triangles, or squares (you can vary the shapes as long as they are all more or less the same thickness).

Beat the egg in a shallow dish and, in another one, mix together the breadcrumbs, herbs (if using), and black pepper.

Dip each chicken shape into the beaten egg so it is covered on all sides, then roll it in the breadcrumb mixture so that it is evenly coated.

Heat the oil or butter in a frying pan. Fry the chicken nuggets for 8 to 12 minutes, turning them as necessary, so that the breadcrumb coating is crisp on all sides and the chicken is thoroughly cooked (cut one nugget in half to check). Serve warm.

Option

• To give your nuggets a tasty cheese-flavored coating, use just 1½ ounces of bread-crumbs and stir in 1 ounce of finely grated parmesan cheese in place of the herbs.

DIPS & SPREADS

Offering your baby soft food as a dip, along with a "dipper" to eat it with, is a great way to help him begin to master the skills he'll need for silverware. Dippers can be foods that a baby can eat (even without teeth), such as breadsticks, or they can be harder foods, which he won't eat but will suck or lick. A stick of celery is ideal because it is similar to a spoon—it can hold a lot of dip and will encourage your baby to use his tongue to scoop it out. Babies can use a spoon to dip with, too—or their fingers. They usually start discovering how dippers work some time around eight months, although some get the hang of it sooner. Be prepared—dips can be very messy when your baby is learning how to eat them.

"Blake's favorite lunch was hummus, carrot sticks, and pita for ages. We started with strips of pita spread with hummus, and then once he discovered how to dunk the pita or carrot in the hummus he was sold. He still loves it."
—Leah, mother of Blake, 19 months

Foods that make good dippers:

- Breadsticks
- Strips or wedges of pita
- Toast fingers
- Sticks of raw vegetable, such as red bell pepper, cucumber, celery, zucchini, and carrot
- Sticks or wedges of fruit, such as apple, nectarine, and mango

Hummus

Hummus is a really nutritious dip, and most babies love it. It can be eaten with warm pita bread—cut into strips or wedges, or halved—or with raw vegetable sticks or breadsticks as dippers. It's lovely with salad, and it makes a tasty filling for baked potatoes. It's also good in sandwiches or on toast. Try it on freshly baked ciabatta bread rolls, with grated carrot and cheese, too.

One 15-ounce can chickpeas (or ½ cup dried chickpeas, precooked—see page 45)
1 or 2 garlic cloves, finely chopped or crushed
Juice of 1 lemon (approx. 4 tablespoons)
Approx. 2 tablespoons tahini
2 to 3 tablespoons olive oil
Pinch of paprika

Rinse and drain the chickpeas and mash them with a potato masher (or use a blender or food processor). Add a little of the garlic, lemon juice, tahini, and olive oil and mix thoroughly.

Taste the hummus to see if it needs more garlic, lemon juice, or tahini; add more oil if you want a smoother texture.

Transfer the hummus to a serving dish and sprinkle with paprika. Chill in the fridge before serving.

Options

• Try adding some ground black pepper or a pinch of cumin along with the garlic and lemon juice.
• Chopped fresh herbs, such as parsley or cilantro, can also be added for a tasty variation.
• Add 1 tablespoon of plain yogurt or sour cream for a creamier dip.

Storage: *Hummus keeps well in the fridge (covered) for 2 to 3 days.*

Guacamole

Guacamole can be served as a dip or as a spread on toast, rice cakes, or soft warm tortillas but it quickly goes brown, so it needs to be eaten within an hour or two.

> **2 ripe medium tomatoes, blanched, skinned and cooled**
> **1 ripe avocado, cut in half, with the pit removed**
> **Juice of 1 lemon (approx. 4 tablespoons)**
> **½ garlic clove, finely chopped or crushed**
> **2 teaspoons sour cream (optional)**
> **1 teaspoon chopped fresh cilantro (optional)**

Chop the tomatoes finely. Scoop the avocado flesh out of the skin, put it into a bowl and mash with a fork. Mix in the lemon juice, garlic, tomatoes and sour cream (if using).

Sprinkle with the chopped cilantro (if using) and serve immediately.

Yogurt and Cucumber Dip

This is the perfect dip to serve with a spicy curry, raw vegetable sticks, or chickpea patties (see page 57).

> **½ medium cucumber, peeled and deseeded**
> **1 cup plain yogurt (preferably with active live cultures)**
> **1 small red onion, finely chopped**
> **1 tablespoon fresh lemon juice (or 1 teaspoon fresh lime juice)**
> **1 to 2 tablespoons chopped fresh cilantro**
> **Freshly ground black pepper**

Tip: *Cucumber is easier to grate when it's in one piece, so if you prefer you can leave the seeds in, then drain it once grated. You can also leave the skin on to provide a bit of extra color and texture.*

Grate the cucumber into a bowl and add the yogurt, onion, lemon (or lime) juice, and cilantro. Stir well, add black pepper to taste, and chill before serving.

Options

- For serving with a curry, add ¼ teaspoon of ground cumin, or a pinch of ground nutmeg, cinnamon, or cardamom.
- For serving with chickpea patties or as a dip, try adding 2 cloves of garlic (finely chopped or crushed) and replacing the cilantro with chopped fresh mint or dill.

Bean Spread

This spread is great as a dip, in sandwiches, or spread on toast or rice cakes.

> One 15-ounce can red kidney beans, lima beans, or green beans (or ½ cup dried beans, precooked—see page 45)
>
> 1 small onion, roughly chopped
>
> 1 medium carrot, cooked
>
> 1 to 2 teaspoons tomato paste
>
> ½ teaspoon dried mixed herbs
>
> 2 teaspoons cider vinegar
>
> 1 to 2 teaspoons oil

Put all the ingredients into a blender or food processor and blend to a smooth paste (or mash thoroughly with a potato masher). Chill before serving.

Salmon Spread

This spread is very nutritious and can be served on toast, oat cakes, or rice cakes, or with a little salad.

> One 5-ounce can salmon (in oil or spring water, not brine), drained thoroughly, with skin and any bones removed
>
> 1 cup ricotta cheese
>
> Juice of ½ lemon (approx. 2 tablespoons)
>
> 2 tablespoons natural yogurt (preferably with active live cultures)
>
> Freshly ground black pepper

Put all the ingredients into a bowl and stir thoroughly until smooth and well combined (or use a blender or food processor).

Option

• You can make a similar spread using canned mackerel, sardines or tuna.

Baba Ganoush (Eggplant Dip)

Baba ganoush is best served as a dip, but it also makes a delicious spread (on toast or rice cakes) or a filling for baked potato.

> **1 medium eggplant (whole)**
> **Juice of 1 lemon (approx. 4 tablespoons)**
> **1 garlic clove, peeled**
> **1 tablespoon tahini (sesame seed paste)**
> **Pinch of chili powder (optional)**
> **Pinch of ground cumin**
> **Pinch of freshly ground black pepper**
> **A little olive oil**
> **2 teaspoons fresh parsley, coarsely chopped**

Preheat the oven to 400°F and lightly grease a baking sheet. Pierce the skin of the eggplant in several places with a fork and put it on the baking sheet. Bake for about 30 to 40 minutes, until the skin has blistered, turning the eggplant over after about 15 minutes to ensure even cooking. Remove from the oven and allow to cool, then peel and put in a colander. Allow to drain thoroughly for 10 to 15 minutes.

Cut the drained eggplant into a few large pieces and put it into a food processor with all the other ingredients, except the olive oil and parsley. Blend thoroughly or use a bowl and a hand-held blender if you prefer.

Chill, then drizzle with olive oil and sprinkle with the parsley before serving.

Options

• Add 1 tablespoon of plain yogurt for a creamier dip.

Soups

Don't be afraid to offer your baby soup, even though it won't be the easiest thing for her to eat at first. Many naturally thick soups, such as butternut squash soup, can be made thicker still, or she may be able to eat it with a dipper (see page 22) or a spoon preloaded by you. Some soups can be left chunky and unblended, so your baby can fish out pieces of food. Or you can add cooked rice, pasta, or small pieces of bread to the soup, to make it easier for her to pick it up in soft handfuls. However, you may need to hold onto your baby's bowl, if she isn't used to using one, or buy one that sticks to the table, so it doesn't get tipped over. Don't forget to check that the soup has cooled down before putting it in front of her.

A large pan of soup takes about the same time to make as a small one, so you might want to make double quantities of these recipes and freeze some for later.

"Ashton used to eat lots of soup just by dipping pieces of bread into it—and by 15 months he'd eat soup by using a spoon half the time and then dunking bread in the rest. He really enjoys his soup." —Jackie, mother of Ashton, 2 years

Thick Butternut Squash Soup

Butternut squash is deliciously sweet and has a soft texture, making it ideal for soups—but you can use any other firm squash or pumpkin for this recipe.

Serves 2 adults and 1 baby

Oil or butter (preferably unsalted) for frying

1 medium onion, finely chopped

1 medium butternut squash, peeled, deseeded, and cubed

1 garlic clove, finely chopped or crushed

1 teaspoon garam masala

1 teaspoon ground cumin (optional)

2½ cups chicken or vegetable stock (low-sodium or homemade, see pages 176–177)

Freshly ground black pepper, to taste

Heat the oil or butter in a large saucepan and fry the onion until just soft. Add the squash, garlic, garam masala, and cumin (if using), and fry gently for a few minutes, stirring so that nothing sticks to the bottom of the pan or burns. Add the stock, bring to a boil, then cover and simmer for 30 minutes.

Check that the squash is soft, then blend to a smooth soup in a blender or food processor and add black pepper to taste. If it isn't thick enough for your baby to manage, cook uncovered for a further 5 to 10 minutes.

Serve warm with chunks of fresh bread or toast.

Options

• Fresh grated ginger or some chili flakes can be added with the garlic to make a spicier soup.

• You can add chunks of carrots or sweet potatoes with the butternut squash to make a more richly flavored soup.

Thick Lentil Soup

This rich soup gets much of its flavor from the chorizo, which is fairly salty, so it's okay to eat occasionally but not every day. It's thick enough for a baby to get quite a lot with a dipper. Chopping the chorizo into thin sticks makes it curly when cooked, which is great fun for babies.

Serves 2 adults and 1 baby

2 ounces chorizo sausage (preferably unsliced)

Oil or butter (preferably unsalted) for frying

½ medium onion, sliced

1 garlic clove, finely chopped or crushed

½ cup red lentils, rinsed thoroughly in cold water and drained

1 bay leaf

2½ cups water, or chicken or vegetable stock (low-sodium or homemade, see pages 176–177)

If your chorizo is unsliced, chop it into thin sticks, approx. 2 inches long.

Heat the oil or butter in a large saucepan and fry the onion until just soft. Add the garlic and chorizo and fry for a few more minutes. Add the lentils and cook for 1 to 2 minutes. Add the bay leaf and top up with enough water or stock to triple the volume of the ingredients in the pan. Bring to a boil, then cover and simmer for 45 minutes, until the lentils are soft. If it is not thick enough, take the lid off and simmer for a further 5 minutes.

Remove the bay leaf and serve warm with chunks of fresh bread or toast.

Chicken Soup

This is a lovely soup to make with the remains of a roast chicken. You can leave the solid ingredients as chunks for your baby to pick up, or you can blend everything to make a smooth soup. You can then either show your baby how to dip bread into it or offer her pieces of soaked bread.

Serves 2 adults and 1 baby

Oil or butter (preferably unsalted) for frying

1 small onion, chopped

1 to 2 garlic cloves, finely chopped or crushed

3 to 4 ounces cooked chicken

1 large carrot, cut to suit your baby

1 small parsnip, cut to suit your baby

1 small celery stick, cut to suit your baby

1 small handful of frozen peas

1 to 2 tablespoons red or French green lentils, rinsed thoroughly in cold water and drained

1 sprig of fresh thyme (or a pinch of dried)

Freshly ground black pepper

3¼ cups chicken or vegetable stock (low-sodium or homemade—see pages 176–177)

Heat the oil or butter in a large saucepan, add the onion, and fry until soft. Add the garlic and fry for another minute or two. Add the cooked chicken, prepared vegetables, peas, lentils, thyme, and black pepper. Pour in the stock and bring to a boil. Reduce the heat, cover, and simmer for 20 minutes.

Blend the soup with a blender or leave it as it is, depending on what is easier for your baby. Serve warm, with chunks of fresh bread.

SALADS

Most salads are full of vitamins and minerals. They are particularly good for babies who are progressing with baby-led weaning because they contain lots of different shapes and textures to pick up, examine, and then test out with gums and teeth.

"Daniela hasn't really worked out what to do with salads yet. She's very interested but she just plays with bits—she'll chew a leaf, but the whole thing will come back out again."
　　　　　　　—Paola, mother of Alessandra, 3 years, and Daniela, 8 months

Raw Salads

Raw salad doesn't have to mean just lettuce, tomato, and cucumber; many vegetables, such as carrots, beets, and zucchini, can be eaten raw (babies can often manage them grated), and fruit such as strawberries and oranges (in segments or chunks) are delicious with a balsamic dressing.

Don't expect your baby to eat lots of raw salad leaves at first, because she won't be able to chew them very effectively—but she will almost certainly want to try. She will, however, probably enjoy sticks of cucumber or red bell pepper.

Raw salad ingredients need to be thoroughly washed. To dry greens, shake them over the sink or inside a clean tea towel, or use a salad spinner.

Cooked Salads

Simple, delicious salads can be made using many different vegetables, eaten warm or at room temperature. When cooked, simply drain them and add a dressing (see page 84). Roasted summer vegetables (see page 143), home-cooked or canned red kidney beans or lima beans, lightly steamed green beans or snap or snow peas, and steamed or boiled potatoes (especially new potatoes) or beets are all great in salads.

You can also make a salad using cold cooked rice, couscous, or bulgur, together with some vegetables or fruit.

Croutons

Croutons go well with many salads and they add yet another texture for your baby to try. They are very easy to make: all you need is one slice of bread per person and about 1 tablespoon of olive oil (preferably extra virgin). Preheat the oven to 400°F. Cut the bread into cubes (with some finger shapes or small triangles for your baby) and put them on a baking sheet. Brush the shapes all over with olive oil, then bake them in the oven for about 5 minutes, until golden brown.

Potato Salad

This is a great salad for babies who are just getting started—you can easily cut the potatoes and cucumber into shapes that your baby will be able to pick up (see page 19), and the crème fraîche makes the mixture sticky, rather than slippery. Potato salad goes particularly well with fish such as salmon and mackerel.

Serves 2 adults and 1 baby

½ cup crème fraîche or sour cream

½ to 1 garlic clove, finely chopped or crushed

1 tablespoon chopped fresh chives

Freshly ground black pepper, to taste

1 pound new potatoes, cooked, cooled and cut to suit your baby

¼ medium cucumber, peeled and cut to suit your baby

Combine the crème fraîche, garlic, chives, and black pepper. Add the cooked potatoes and cucumber and stir well. As this salad contains crème fraîche and garlic, it can be served as it is, without any additional dressing.

Options

• Adults may prefer to chop their cucumber into small chunks, rather than sticks. If you want to do this, simply add the cucumber in sticks to your baby's portion, and the chopped cucumber to the rest.

• You can swap the chives for a little chopped dill or parsley.

Roast Carrot, Bean, and Feta Salad

This salad offers lots of different shapes for your baby to explore. If she is just starting to pick up things with her thumb and forefinger (the pincer grip) lima beans are ideal to practice with; if she's a BLW beginner she'll enjoy the baby carrots and green beans.

Serves 2 adults and 1 baby

2 tablespoons olive oil

1 pound small whole baby carrots (cut any larger ones in half lengthwise)

1 sprig of fresh lemon thyme (optional)

Freshly ground black pepper, to taste

¼ pound haricot verts (French green beans), trimmed and cut in half

Half of a 15-ounce can lima or cannellini beans, rinsed and drained (2 ounces dried beans, precooked—see page 45)

½ small red onion, finely sliced

½ cup feta cheese, crumbled

1 small bunch of fresh mint, chopped

Preheat the oven to 425°F. Put half the oil into a large roasting pan and heat, in the oven. Put the carrots into the roasting pan with the lemon thyme (if using). Toss the carrots to coat them with the oil, sprinkle them with black pepper, then roast in the oven for 20 to 30 minutes until the carrots are tender, turning them halfway through cooking.

Meanwhile, steam the green beans for about 5 minutes until tender. Drain, rinse immediately with cold water, then drain thoroughly.

Mix together the green beans, lima, or cannellini beans, remaining oil, onion, and feta, and add black pepper to taste. Mix in the hot carrots, then sprinkle with the mint just before serving.

Serve as it is, or with a dressing of your choice (see page 84).

Option

• You can use ricotta salata instead of feta; it has a similar texture but is less salty.

Chicken Caesar Salad

This Caesar salad is made with strips of chicken, which are ideal for babies just starting out. The anchovies that are traditionally included in a Caesar dressing are too salty for babies, but adults may like to add them to their portion. The basic French dressing (see page 84) is an integral part of this recipe, so we've repeated it here.

Serves 2 adults and 1 baby

Oil or butter (preferably unsalted) for frying

2 or 3 chicken breasts, cut into strips

2 heads (or hearts) crispy lettuce (such as romaine), washed and drained

2 handfuls of croutons (see page 76)

½ cup grated or thinly sliced Parmesan cheese

For the dressing:
1 garlic clove, finely chopped or crushed

2 tablespoons olive oil (preferably extra virgin)

2 teaspoons lemon juice or white wine vinegar

Freshly ground black pepper, to taste

Heat the oil or butter in a frying pan and fry the chicken strips for 5 to 10 minutes, turning occasionally, until cooked through (check by cutting one in half), then drain on paper towels and set aside.

Thoroughly mix together all the dressing ingredients and put into a large bowl. Toss the lettuce leaves in the dressing. Add the chicken strips and croutons and mix lightly.

You can serve this salad with the chicken warm or you can use cold, precooked chicken breast from a rotisserie or oven-roasted chicken. No additional dressing is needed. Divide among individual plates and top with Parmesan cheese.

Orange and Watercress Salad

This recipe uses a dressing made with cider vinegar, which goes especially well with oranges. Chicory has a very distinctive, bitter flavor that your baby might enjoy trying. This salad is ideal for babies with a little dexterity, but even a baby who's just beginning to feed herself will enjoy picking up the orange segments and will get a taste of the orange combined with the dressing.

Serves 2 adults and 1 baby

1 orange
1 head baby chicory, washed and drained
2 ounces watercress
1 tablespoon chopped fresh cilantro (optional)

For the dressing:
2 tablespoons olive oil (preferably extra virgin)
2 teaspoons cider vinegar
Freshly ground black pepper, to taste

Peel the orange carefully, removing all the pith. Either cut the flesh into chunks or separate it into segments (if you can, remove the thin skin from each segment). Try to catch any orange juice that escapes, to add to the dressing.

Separate the chicory leaves and break the watercress into short pieces.

Thoroughly mix together the dressing ingredients, plus any collected orange juice, and put into a large bowl. Add the orange, chicory, and watercress and toss them in the dressing. Sprinkle with the chopped cilantro and serve.

This salad goes well with cold chicken or pork. It needs no additional dressing.

Option

• If you find chicory too bitter, you can use another crisp lettuce like romaine instead.

Tuscan Salad

The roasted peppers in this recipe are deliciously sweet and soft. They are also quite slippery, providing your baby with lots of practice at dealing with a tricky texture to hold onto. The beans are good for when she's learning to pick things up with her thumb and finger (the pincer grip).

Serves 2 adults and 1 baby

1 red bell pepper, deseeded and cut into 6 to 8 long strips

1 yellow bell pepper, deseeded and cut into 6 to 8 long strips

6 ounces bread, preferably ciabatta or another crusty bread

French dressing with garlic (see page 84) (optional)

3 ripe fresh plum tomatoes, cut into quarters

One 15-ounce can cannellini beans, rinsed and drained (or ½ cup dried beans, precooked—see page 45)

3 or 4 black olives (in oil, not brine), pits removed and thinly sliced

Handful of fresh basil leaves, torn

Preheat the broiler. Broil the peppers, skin-side-up, for about 5 minutes, so that all the skin is thoroughly charred, then allow to cool. When cool, remove the skins and cut the flesh into strips.

Cut the bread into rough fingers for your baby and smaller cubes for the adults and broil, turning once, until lightly toasted (or use a toaster and cut after toasting).

Put the dressing (if using) into a salad bowl; add the roasted peppers, tomatoes, beans, olives and basil, and toss well. Top with the toasted bread.

Tuscan salad goes well with goat cheese or Brie.

Options

- If your baby can manage them, a couple of tablespoons of toasted pine nuts make a tasty addition and provide a different texture. (It's probably best to avoid Chinese and Korean pine nuts as these can occasionally leave a bitter aftertaste.)
- Capers are delicious with this salad but they tend to be salty, so they are not really suitable for babies—but you may like to add them to your own plate.

Goat Cheese Salad

Goat cheese has a very distinctive flavor that may be interesting for your baby to try—and there's plenty here for babies who are just starting out, including soft, roasted peppers without their skins.

Serves 2 adults and 1 baby

1 red bell pepper, deseeded and cut into 6 to 8 long strips

7 ounces soft goat cheese (sometimes labeled chèvre—usually about 3 inches in diameter)

4 slices bread

A little olive oil

Freshly ground black pepper

Approx. 2 tablespoons salad dressing (French dressing with added garlic works well—see page 84)

2 or 3 handfuls mixed green salad leaves, washed and drained (e.g. lettuce, arugula, watercress, spinach)

Preheat the broiler. Broil the pepper, skin-side up, for about 5 minutes so that all the skin is thoroughly charred, then allow to cool.

Cut the cheese into four thin slices and use a biscuit cutter to cut the bread into circles roughly the same diameter as the cheese. Toast the bread on both sides, then put a piece of cheese on top of each slice.

Drizzle a little olive oil and some black pepper (to taste) onto the cheese and broil for about 2 minutes or until toasted.

Meanwhile, skin the peppers and cut them into strips. Put the dressing into a salad bowl, add the salad leaves and strips of pepper, and toss them in the dressing.

Put the salad on a wide flat plate and arrange the slices of goat cheese toasts on the top. Serve while the goat cheese is still warm. The toast can be cut into wedge or finger shapes for your baby.

Colorful Stir-Fry Salad

This delicious salad has lots of different colors, textures, and tastes for your baby to explore, and is particularly good for babies whose teeth are appearing and who are beginning to enjoy crunchy textures.

Serves 2 adults and 1 baby

2 handfuls mixed salad leaves, washed and drained (e.g. lettuce, arugula, watercress, spinach, or mizuna)

½ orange bell pepper, deseeded and cut into thin sticks

½ yellow bell pepper, deseeded and cut into thin sticks

6 cherry tomatoes, cut in half

½ medium avocado, pit removed

A little light sesame oil for frying

½ tablespoon mustard seeds (optional)

6 whole baby corn, cut in half lengthwise

1 medium beet (raw), peeled and cut into thin sticks

1 medium carrot, cut into thin sticks

Put the salad leaves into a large salad bowl and add the peppers and tomatoes.

Cut the avocado flesh into strips, leaving some of the skin on to make it easier for your baby to grip. Add to the bowl with the peppers and tomatoes.

Heat a wok or a deep, nonstick frying pan until very hot and add the oil and mustard seeds (if using). When the seeds start to pop, add the baby corn, beet, and carrot, and stir-fry for a few minutes. Keep the pan very hot and keep stirring the vegetables. Cook until just tender (or a little softer if your baby has no teeth yet), then add to the salad bowl.

This salad is especially good served with a helping of croutons and a little extra sesame oil.

Option

• 1 tablespoon of toasted sesame seeds added to the salad gives a distinctive flavor.

Cheesy Tuna and Corn Pasta Salad

This is a great BLW dish as the tuna and cheese stick to the pasta, so it's easy to eat. And once your baby is developing her pincer grip she will enjoy practicing it on the pieces of corn.

Serves 2 adults and 1 baby

8 ounces pasta (fusilli works best)

One 5-ounce can tuna (low-sodium, in oil or spring water)

One 8-ounce can corn

4 tablespoons cream cheese or mascarpone

Cook the pasta in a pan of boiling water according to the package instructions, then drain, rinse with cold water, drain again, and allow to cool.

Meanwhile, break the tuna into flakes, add the corn and cream cheese, and mix well. Add the cooled pasta and stir to combine. Serve immediately or put in the fridge until later.

This dish should be served cold and is good with extra cucumber sticks, sliced bell peppers (red, orange, yellow, or green), and tomato wedges (or halved cherry tomatoes).

Salad Dressings

Most salads can be served with just a little good-quality extra virgin olive oil and a sprinkling of black pepper, but many can be transformed by a good dressing. The basic dressings below will go with most salads. An easy way to mix the ingredients is to put everything into a small jar, put the lid on, and shake vigorously. (The oil will separate out between uses—just shake to remix.)

Salad dressings will usually keep for a week or two in the fridge, so it's a good idea to make up enough for several salads in one go.

Note: Mayonnaise is not recommended for babies because most brands contain raw egg; however, egg-free mayonnaise is available in some larger supermarkets or health-food stores.

Lemon and Oil Dressing

Combine 2 tablespoons olive oil (preferably extra virgin) with the juice of 1 lemon (approx. 4 tablespoons). If you like, you can add 1 or 2 teaspoons chopped fresh mint or a little grated fresh ginger.

French Dressing

Combine 2 tablespoons olive oil (preferably extra virgin) with 2 teaspoons lemon juice or white (or red) wine vinegar and some freshly ground black pepper to taste. You can also add 1 teaspoon Dijon or wholegrain mustard, 1 or 2 crushed garlic cloves or a couple of teaspoons of chopped fresh herbs, such as chives, mint or parsley, and thyme.

Balsamic Dressing

Combine 2 tablespoons balsamic vinegar with 3 to 4 tablespoons olive oil (preferably extra virgin) and, if you like, 1 tablespoon finely chopped fresh basil or cilantro.

Creamy Onion Dressing

Combine 5 fluid ounces sour cream or plain yogurt with 2 tablespoons white wine vinegar, ¼ finely chopped onion, and a pinch of freshly ground black pepper. (This dressing goes especially well with a potato salad or with a grated carrot or shredded cabbage, as a coleslaw.)

MAINS: MEAT

Meat is an easy first food for your baby—especially if it's tender. Stews and slow-cooked dishes are ideal, and homemade sausages, burgers, and patties are easy for babies to pick up and chew.

Homemade Beef Burgers

These tasty burgers are much healthier than the fast-food version and can be cut into wedges when cooked to make them easy for your baby to handle. Serve with hamburger buns or English muffins, sliced tomato, raw onion, and Spicy Tomato Salsa (see page 148). They're also good with potato wedges or couscous, and salad.

Serves 2 adults and 1 baby

1 pound lean ground beef
1 small onion, finely chopped
1 egg, beaten
1 teaspoon Dijon mustard (optional)
1 tablespoon chopped fresh parsley or cilantro (optional)
Oil for frying (if needed)

Put all the ingredients into a bowl and mix thoroughly. Shape the mixture into balls about the size of tennis balls (flouring or wetting your hands will help to keep it from sticking), then flatten them into burgers, making sure they are all roughly the same thickness. If you have time, cover the burgers and put them in the fridge to firm up for an hour or so (or until you're ready to cook them).

Heat a griddle or frying pan, with oil if needed, and fry the burgers for 5 to 8 minutes on each side, pressing them down if griddling, until cooked through (check by cutting one in half—there should be no pink meat). Serve warm.

Beef and Broccoli Stir-Fry

"Lucien has still only got two teeth, but he'll suck on strips or chunks of meat, chew it, and spit bits out. For a couple of weeks he hardly wanted anything but meat."
—Jane, mother of Lucien, 11 months

This stir-fry has just the right shapes for your baby when he's starting out, and it's quick to cook—you don't have to marinate the beef if you are in a hurry. (Remember to wash your hands after handling the raw chili pepper, because chili juice can burn.)

Serves 2 adults and 1 baby

10 ounces lean beef steak

2 garlic cloves, finely chopped or crushed

1½-inch piece of fresh ginger, peeled and finely sliced

¼ red chili pepper, chopped (deseeded and veins removed) or dried chili flakes, to taste (optional)

3 to 4 scallions, finely sliced

1 tablespoon chopped fresh cilantro (optional)

1 tablespoon sesame oil

6 to 8 broccoli florets, halved

Oil for frying

Cut the beef into thin strips and put them into a large bowl.

Add the garlic, ginger, chili, scallions, and half of the cilantro (if using). Add the sesame oil and stir well. Cover and leave to marinate for a couple of hours.

Lightly steam the broccoli. Heat a wok or a deep, nonstick frying pan until very hot and add a little oil. Transfer the marinated ingredients to the wok and add the broccoli.

Stir-fry for 2 or 3 minutes, keeping the pan very hot all the time.

Sprinkle with the remaining cilantro and serve immediately (cooled for your baby) with noodles or rice, accompanied by green vegetables.

Option

• Adults may prefer this dish with some soy sauce or tamari. Simply take your baby's portion out when the beef and vegetables are cooked and then add the extra sauce to the rest, stirring briefly.

Weeknight Chili

This is a real favorite with many families—filling, tasty, and easy to make. Although it's made with ground beef, rather than chunks, it's surprisingly adaptable, even for the early days of BLW when your baby needs large pieces of food to grab. Simply allow the meat to stay in large clumps, rather than breaking them up, and your baby will be able to get hold of them and take them to his mouth. Cutting the onions into wedges will make the pieces easier to grab, too. Go easy on the chili flakes the first time you make it, until you know how hot your baby likes it. Chili tastes better if it's kept in the fridge overnight and eaten the next day, so this is worth bearing in mind when you're planning your meals. Be sure to reheat it thoroughly before serving.

Serves 2 adults and 1 baby, generously

Oil for frying

2 medium onions, cut into wedges or chopped

9 ounces lean ground beef

¼ teaspoon to ½ teaspoon crushed dried chili flakes (or chili powder), to taste

1 garlic clove, finely chopped or crushed

½ teaspoon ground cumin

1 small carrot, grated (optional)

1 celery stick, finely chopped (optional)

One 14-ounce can tomatoes, chopped

One 15-ounce can red kidney beans, drained and rinsed (or approx. ½ cup dried beans, precooked—see page 45)

Heat the oil in a large saucepan, add the onions, and fry until just beginning to soften. Add the meat to the pan and cook until browned, turning as necessary and allowing the meat to stay in large clumps. Add the chili flakes, garlic, cumin, carrot, and celery (if using) and allow to cook for another minute or two.

Add the tomatoes, stir well, cover, and simmer for 35 to 40 minutes.

Add the kidney beans and stir well. Cook for a further 10 minutes, to allow the beans to heat through.

Serve warm, with rice (or couscous) and a salad. Sour cream or guacamole on the side is good, too—and you may like to have some cooling plain yogurt on hand in case you have made it a little too spicy for your baby.

Beef and Onion Stew

"We eat lots of stews—Harry likes to see what he's got and to pick out the bits he wants. He still doesn't like things mixed together too much."

—Alison, mother of Harry, 2 years

Serves 2 adults and 1 baby

Oil for frying

2 medium onions, cut into wedges

12 ounces lean beef chuck roast, cut to suit your baby

1 medium carrot, cut to suit your baby

2 cups beef or vegetable stock (low-sodium or homemade, see pages 176–177)

1 bouquet garni (a few sprigs of fresh parsley, thyme, and a bay leaf tied together with kitchen twine)

Freshly ground black pepper, to taste

Approx. 1 tablespoon cornstarch

Heat the oil in a pan and add the onions and beef pieces. Fry gently, turning the meat occasionally until the beef is browned on all sides and the onion is beginning to soften. Add the carrot, stock, bouquet garni, and black pepper, and bring to a boil. Cover and simmer for 1 to 2 hours, until the meat is tender.

When you are almost ready to serve the stew, remove the bouquet garni and turn up the heat slightly. Remove 2 tablespoons of the stock and mix to a smooth paste with the cornstarch. Add a further few tablespoons of stock, then return the stock plus cornstarch to the pan and cook for 3 to 5 minutes, stirring gently, until the sauce thickens.

Serve warm with dumplings (see page 146) or bread, potatoes, and green vegetables.

Option

• You can add mushrooms, potato, rutabaga, or turnip, along with (or instead of) the carrot. Sweet potato, squash, and zucchini are also good—add them a bit later so they don't disintegrate.

Goulash

This traditional Hungarian dish is based on slow-cooked beef, which is easy for a baby to chew, so it's good for beginners. If you want to include more vegetables you can add sliced carrots, potatoes, or parsnips before it goes into the oven.

Serves 2 adults and 1 baby

Oil for frying

1 medium onion, cut into wedges

½ green bell pepper, deseeded and cut to suit your baby

12 ounces lean beef chuck roast, cut to suit your baby

1 or 2 teaspoons paprika

2 tablespoons tomato paste

2 tablespoons all-purpose flour

Pinch of grated nutmeg

Pinch of freshly ground black pepper

1 cup beef or vegetable stock (low-sodium or homemade, see pages 176–177)

1 large tomato, skinned and roughly chopped

1 bouquet garni (a few sprigs of fresh parsley, thyme, and a bay leaf tied together with kitchen twine)

½ cup sour cream (optional)

1 tablespoon fresh parsley or chives, chopped (optional)

Preheat the oven to 325°F. Heat the oil in a pan, add the onion and bell pepper, and fry until they begin to soften. Add the beef and cook for 3 to 5 minutes, until browned all over. Add the paprika and cook gently for 1 minute. Stir in the tomato paste, flour, nutmeg and black pepper, and cook for 3 more minutes.

Add half the stock, the tomato, and bouquet garni, and bring to a boil. Stir until thickened, then add more stock until the sauce is the consistency you want. Transfer the mixture to an ovenproof casserole (with a lid) and bake for 1½ to 2 hours.

Remove the bouquet garni, swirl in the sour cream (if using), and sprinkle with chopped parsley or chives (if using) before serving. Serve warm with dumplings made with 1 teaspoon caraway seeds (see page 146), potatoes or rice, and vegetables.

Meatloaf

Meatloaf is a great dish for baby-led weaning, as it holds together perfectly when cooked and is soft and moist to eat. You can adapt the seasoning to suit your taste, or add a dash of Worcestershire sauce to give it extra flavor.

Serves 2 adults and 1 baby, generously

Oil, for greasing

1 pound lean ground beef

3 to 4 ounces good-quality sausage meat (or squeeze the meat out of your favorite sausages)

1 medium onion, finely chopped

2 tablespoons tomato paste (optional)

1 cup fresh breadcrumbs

1 teaspoon dried mixed herbs

Freshly ground black pepper, to taste

1 medium carrot, grated (optional)

1 celery stick, finely chopped (optional)

1 egg, beaten

Preheat the oven to 350°F and lightly grease a 9 × 5-inch loaf pan.

Put the beef, sausage, onion, tomato paste (if using), breadcrumbs, herbs, black pepper, carrot, and celery (if using) into a large bowl and mix well.

Add the egg and mix thoroughly, using your hands to squeeze the mixture (flouring or wetting them first will help to keep it from sticking). Transfer the mixture to the loaf pan. Press down well and cover with foil.

Bake in the oven for about 1 hour, or until the loaf begins to come away from the sides of the pan.

Remove from the pan before slicing and serving warm with green vegetables or salad. If you're planning to eat it cold, allow to cool before slicing.

Options

• Use a blender or food processor if you want the meatloaf really smooth.

• Leftovers can be mixed with a tomato-based sauce and served with pasta.

Meatballs in Tomato Sauce

Meatballs are very easy for babies to grip, and nice and soft to eat.

Serves 2 adults and 1 baby

For the meatballs:

1 pound lean ground beef

1 egg, beaten

2 or 3 garlic cloves, finely chopped
  or crushed

1 teaspoon dried mixed herbs or
  oregano

2 tablespoons chopped fresh parsley

1 tablespoon balsamic vinegar

½ cup breadcrumbs (1 slice of bread)

Oil for frying (if needed)

For the sauce:

1 medium onion, finely chopped

1 or 2 garlic cloves, chopped

1 tablespoon tomato paste

One 14-ounce can chopped or
  crushed tomatoes

1 handful fresh basil leaves, torn

Pinch of freshly ground black
  pepper, to taste

Put all the meatball ingredients except the oil into a bowl and combine using your hands (or use a food processor). Shape the mixture into balls the size of golf balls (flouring or wetting your hands first will help to keep it from sticking). If you have time, put them in the fridge to firm up for an hour or so.

Heat the oil in a frying pan, add the meatballs, and fry gently until they are browned all over, turning as necessary. Lift the meatballs out of the pan with a slotted spoon (to drain off the oil) and set aside. Return the pan to the heat and add the onion. Fry gently for a few minutes, then add the garlic and cook until the onion is soft. Stir in the tomato paste, then add the tomatoes, half the basil, and the black pepper. Stir well and bring to a boil. Return the meatballs to the pan, cover, and simmer for 10 to 15 minutes until the sauce has thickened and the meatballs are cooked through (test one by cutting in half—there should be no pink meat).

Serve warm, with pasta, rice, or couscous, with the remaining basil sprinkled on top.

Options

• If you like you can replace the canned tomatoes with 6 to 8 ripe plum tomatoes (or about 15 cherry tomatoes), blanched, peeled, and chopped.
• Try making meatballs from ground lamb or pork, or half pork and half beef.
• Adding 1 tablespoon of Parmesan cheese to the meatball mixture will give extra flavor.

Shepherd's Pie

This is traditional family comfort food—perfect for cold winter evenings. Your baby will be able to manage this dish once he can open his fist on purpose and no longer needs to have sticks of food poking out. If he's not quite there yet, serve it with sticks of steamed vegetables and let him have some of the shepherd's pie to play with.

Serves 2 adults and 1 baby

1 pound starchy potatoes, peeled and cut into chunks

Approx. ½ cup milk

2 medium carrots, sliced

1 stick of celery, chopped

1½ cups lamb or vegetable stock (low-sodium or homemade, see pages 176–177)

Oil for frying

1 medium onion, finely chopped

10 ounces lean ground lamb

1 tablespoon all-purpose flour

1 tablespoon tomato paste

Splash of Worcestershire sauce (optional)

1 tablespoon chopped fresh rosemary or thyme (or 1 teaspoon dried rosemary or thyme)

½ cup frozen peas

2 tablespoons butter (preferably unsalted)

½ cup grated cheese (optional)

Freshly ground black pepper, to taste

Preheat the oven to 350°F. Put the potatoes in a pan with enough milk to come almost halfway up the potatoes. Bring to a boil, cover, and simmer for 20 to 30 minutes until soft.

Meanwhile, put the carrots, celery, and stock into another pan and bring to a boil. Cover and simmer until the vegetables are just tender, then lift them out with a slotted spoon and set aside, reserving the stock for later.

Heat the oil in a large pan and cook the onion until soft. Add the ground lamb and cook for 3 to 5 minutes, turning frequently. Break up any clumps as you go (or leave them, to make the meat easier for your baby to grab.)

Stir in the flour, making sure it doesn't form lumps, and gradually add half the stock, stirring constantly. Add the tomato paste and Worcestershire sauce (if using) and stir. Add the vegetables, rosemary or thyme, and peas, and mix well.

Bring the mixture to a boil, reduce the heat, and simmer gently for 10 minutes. Add more of the stock as the mixture thickens, until you get the consistency you want.

Add the butter to the potatoes and the milk in which they were cooked, and mash well.

Transfer the meat mixture into an ovenproof dish and spread the mashed potato over the top. Sprinkle with the grated cheese and some black pepper and put the dish into the oven. Bake for 25 to 30 minutes.

Serve warm, with vegetables.

Option

• Although true shepherd's pie is made with lamb, this recipe also works well with ground beef (called cottage pie). If using beef, replace the rosemary with dried mixed herbs and the lamb stock with homemade or low-sodium beef (or vegetable) stock.

Lamb and Mint Sausages

Store-bought sausages normally need to have their skins removed so that babies can manage them safely. These sausages have no skins, and the shape is perfect for babies starting out. If you have time, put them in the fridge to firm up for an hour or so before you cook them. These are best fried but can also be oven-baked.

Serves 2 adults and 1 baby

½ cup peas
½ medium leek, finely chopped
9 ounces ground lamb
2 teaspoons chopped fresh mint (or 1 teaspoon dried)
1 teaspoon dried mixed herbs
Freshly ground black pepper, to taste
Oil for frying (optional)

Steam, boil, or microwave the peas and leek, then drain. Blend or mash thoroughly, to make a purée. Add the lamb and mix well. Add the herbs and black pepper and stir well.

Shape the mixture into small sausage shapes to suit your baby (flouring or wetting your hands will help to keep it from sticking).

Heat a frying pan, with a little oil, if needed. Fry the sausages for about 10 minutes, turning occasionally, until cooked through (test by cutting in half—there should be no pink meat). Alternatively, put them on a greased baking sheet and bake in the oven at 425°F for about 25 minutes.

Lamb Tagine

This Moroccan dish is traditionally cooked slowly on the stove top in a special pot called a tagine, but a covered pan or casserole placed in the oven will do. Alternatively, you can use a slow cooker. The sweetness of the apricots with the tender lamb and rich mix of spices will give your baby a delicious new range of tastes to discover.

Don't be put off if you don't have all the spices listed below—you'll still be able to make a tasty dish with a combination of those you do have.

Serves 2 adults and 1 baby

Oil for frying

1 medium onion, cut into wedges or finely chopped

2 garlic cloves, finely chopped or crushed

1½-inch piece of fresh ginger, peeled and grated or chopped

10 ounces lean lamb shoulder, cut into strips

1 teaspoon paprika

1 teaspoon turmeric

1 teaspoon ground cinnamon

1 teaspoon coriander seeds, crushed

¼ teaspoon cayenne pepper

Pinch of saffron (optional)

Pinch of freshly ground black pepper

2 to 3 medium tomatoes, roughly chopped (or half of a 14-ounce can tomatoes, drained and chopped)

6 to 8 dried apricots or prunes

1 tablespoon golden or dark raisins

1 cup lamb or vegetable stock (low-sodium or homemade, see pages 176–177)

1 tablespoon chopped fresh cilantro (optional)

Preheat the oven to 325°F. Heat the oil (preferably in a flame-proof casserole so you don't have to transfer the food at the next stage) and add the onion. Fry gently until soft. Add the garlic and ginger, and cook for another minute or two. Add the lamb and continue frying gently until the pieces are browned on all sides.

Mix together all the dried spices and the black pepper, and add them to the pan. Fry for a couple of minutes. Add the tomatoes and dried fruit and heat through.

Put a lid on the casserole (or transfer the ingredients from the pan to a casserole) and add enough stock to almost cover the other ingredients. Put the casserole in the oven and cook for about 2 hours, giving it a stir about halfway through.

Sprinkle with fresh cilantro (if using) before serving, warm, with couscous or rice (with a squeeze of lemon or lime juice) and steamed green beans or salad.

Spicy Lamb Patties

These delicious patties melt in the mouth—perfect for babies who are just starting out. If you don't have time to prepare the cardamom pods and cloves, you can add 2 teaspoons ready-ground cardamom and 1 teaspoon ground cloves instead.

Serves 2 adults and 1 baby

12 to 15 cardamom pods

8 cloves

1 pound lean ground lamb

1¾-inch piece of fresh ginger, peeled and grated or finely chopped

½ teaspoon turmeric

½ teaspoon ground cumin

Approx. ½ teaspoon chili powder, according to taste (optional)

½ cup breadcrumbs (1 slice of bread)

1 egg, beaten

2 tablespoons thick (Greek-style) plain yogurt

Oil for frying (optional)

Use a knife to split open the cardamom pods and put the seeds into a mortar with the cloves (discard the pods). Grind to a powder. (This can also be done using a spice grinder.)

Transfer the powder to a large bowl and add all the remaining ingredients except the egg, yogurt, and oil. Mix well. Add the egg and yogurt and mix thoroughly, so that everything is bound together.

Shape the mixture into small patties (flouring or wetting your hands will help to keep it from sticking), making sure they are all roughly the same thickness. If you have time, cover them and put them in the fridge to firm up for an hour or so.

Heat a frying pan, and add a little oil, if needed. Fry the patties for 5 to 10 minutes on each side, until cooked through and browned.

Serve warm with salad, couscous and roasted vegetables, or rice.

Toad-in-the-Hole

This traditional British favorite is akin to a large popover stuffed with sausages.

Serves 2 adults and 1 baby, generously

1 cup all-purpose flour

Pinch of freshly ground black pepper (optional)

1 to 2 eggs (2 make a richer batter)

1½ cups milk (or half water and half milk)

3 tablespoons olive oil

6 to 8 good-quality medium or small sausages (preferably with herbs)

Put the flour into a mixing bowl and add the black pepper (if using). Make a well in the center and break the egg(s) into it. Pour in half the milk (or the milk and water mixture). Beat or whisk the ingredients together, starting in the middle and gradually working in the flour.

Gradually add the rest of the liquid and continue beating until any remaining lumps have disappeared. If you have used 2 eggs, the consistency should be like heavy cream or pancake batter. Put the mixture in the fridge to rest for at least 15 minutes. Meanwhile, preheat the oven to 425°F.

Pour the olive oil into a shallow roasting pan (approx. 9 × 13 inches) and put it in the oven until the oil is smoking hot.

Arrange the sausages in the pan, evenly spaced, and pour the batter around them.

Return the pan to the oven and bake for 25 to 30 minutes, until the batter is risen and golden. (Don't be tempted to open the oven door in the early stages as it could make the batter collapse.)

Toad-in-the-Hole is best eaten straight from the oven (cooled for your baby). Remove sausage skins from your baby's portion and serve with vegetables of your choice, preferably steamed.

Option

• Add up to 1 tablespoon of mustard to the batter mixture to give it an extra kick.

Tip: *Cutting your baby's sausage in half lengthwise once cooked will help it to cool more quickly and make it easier for him to pick up.*

Classic Roast Dinner

Roast dinners—with plenty of vegetables and homemade gravy—are classic family meals. Served with the traditional British side dish Yorkshire puddings (see page 99) and horseradish sauce (with beef), apple sauce (with pork), mint sauce (with lamb), or stuffing (with chicken), a roast dinner will give your baby plenty of flavors to try.

Potatoes and vegetables, such as sweet potato, carrots, and parsnips, can be roasted (see page 144) with the meat; other vegetables, stuffings, sauces, gravy, and Yorkshire puddings can be cooked while the meat is "resting."

Serves 2 adults and 1 baby, generously

One 2½- to 3-pound roast, more if on the bone, or 1 small chicken (preferably organic)

Potatoes for roasting (optional)

2 whole heads garlic (unpeeled), cut in half

Approx. 2 tablespoons oil (less if the meat has a good covering of fat)

A little freshly ground black pepper

For beef: **a small bunch of fresh thyme, rosemary, bay, and/or sage**

For pork: **a small bunch of fresh thyme, rosemary, and/or sage**

For lamb: **a small bunch of fresh rosemary and/or mint**

For chicken: **2 unwaxed lemons, halved; 4 tablespoons butter (preferably unsalted) or 2 to 3 tablespoons oil; a small bunch of fresh rosemary, and 6 bay leaves**

Take the meat out of the fridge half an hour before you want to cook it.

For chicken, check there is no bag of giblets in the cavity. If you want to stuff it (see page 99), do this now. Alternatively, pierce two of the lemon halves several times with a knife and put them inside the cavity, together with one of the bay leaves, a few sprigs of the rosemary, and half a bulb of garlic. Rub butter or oil all over the breast and legs.

For crispy crackling on pork, use a sharp knife to score the skin deeply into narrow strips, then rub it with oil.

Weigh the meat (including stuffing, if any) and calculate how long you need to cook it for (see page 98). Preheat the oven to at least 375°F.

If roasting potatoes, put them into the roasting pan with the (remaining) garlic and herbs (and, for chicken, the other lemon halves) and coat them with a thin layer of the oil. Put the meat in the middle of the pan, keeping the fatty or buttered side up, and add black pepper. Cover the pan with foil and put it into the center of the oven. Leave to cook for the recommended time. Meanwhile, you can prepare any vegetables for steaming or boiling or make your Yorkshire pudding batter and stuffing mix (if serving separately).

> **Tips:** *If the cooking time of the meat is longer than 1½ hours, put the potatoes in the oven a little later, so they don't overcook.*
>
> *You can use leftover meat in dishes such as curries, rissoles, salads, and soups. Any bones can be used for meat stock (see page 176).*

About 30 minutes before the end of the cooking time, remove the foil. Baste the meat and the potatoes with the hot fat from the roasting pan.

To check the meat is cooked, push a skewer into the thickest part (for chicken, this is the thigh) and check the juice that runs out. For pork and chicken, the juices should be completely clear; lamb and beef can safely be eaten slightly "rare" in the middle, so the juices may appear pink, but not red. *If in doubt, cook it for a bit longer.* (You may need to take out the roast potatoes so they don't burn.)

When the meat is cooked, lift it out of the pan (discarding the garlic), and put it on a chopping board or carving dish. Cover with foil and a dish towel and let it "rest" for 30 minutes (to make it tender and easy to carve). Meanwhile, return the potatoes to the bottom of the oven, cook any Yorkshire puddings, stuffing (if separate), and/or other vegetables, and use the juices from the roasting pan to make "real" gravy (see page 100). Aim for everything to be ready when the meat has finished resting.

Oven roasting times for meat

Type of meat	Oven temperature	Minutes per pound	Plus additional minutes
Beef or lamb	375 to 425°F	25 to 30	25
Pork	375 to 425°F	30 to 35	30
Chicken	375 to 400°F	20	20

Note: The "additional minutes" in the last column are to give the heat time to reach the meat and kick-start the cooking process. Meat must be completely unfrozen before it is cooked, to prevent food poisoning. If in doubt, cook it for longer than usual on a slow heat.

To Make a Simple Stuffing . . .

9 ounces good quality pork sausage

1 small onion, finely chopped

1½ cups fresh breadcrumbs

1 egg, beaten

1 tablespoon fresh sage, chopped (or 1 teaspoon dried)

Freshly ground black pepper, to taste

Combine all the ingredients and mix well with a fork (or food processor).

Either use to stuff a chicken (before cooking), by pushing the mixture loosely into the large opening, or shape the mixture into balls, place them on a small, lightly greased roasting pan and cook them in the oven for about 30 minutes.

To Make Yorkshire Puddings . . .

Makes approximately 12 puddings

1 cup all-purpose flour

2 medium eggs or 1 large egg

1 cup plus 2 tablespoons milk (or milk with a little water, for lighter puddings)

Oil for cooking

> **Tip:** *This batter recipe can also be used for Toad-in-the-Hole (see page 96) or to make rich pancakes (see page 53). You can keep it in the fridge for a couple of days; if it thickens, just stir in a little extra milk or water.*

Preheat the oven to 425°F. Sift the flour into a bowl and make a well in the center. Break the eggs into the flour and add half the milk.

Beat or whisk the ingredients together vigorously. Gradually add the rest of the liquid and continue beating until all lumps have disappeared. Put the batter into the fridge for 20 to 30 minutes.

Put a little oil into each section of a muffin tin and heat in the oven until smoking hot.

Beat the batter mixture again and pour 1 or 2 tablespoons into each well (don't fill them—the puddings will expand considerably during cooking). Put the tin in the top of the oven and bake for 10 to 15 minutes until the puddings are puffy and golden brown. Don't open the oven door too soon or they'll sink!

Serve straight from the oven.

To Make Real Gravy . . .

This is just the best gravy to serve with a meat roast—and much more tasty than gravy made with commercial gravy mixes, which contain a lot of salt. The quantities of ingredients, and the amount of gravy made, will depend on how much meat juice there is and how thick you like your gravy.

> **The juices from the roasting pan in which the meat has cooked**
> **A few tablespoons all-purpose flour**
> **Hot low-sodium or homemade meat or vegetable stock (see**
>   **pages 176–177, or if you have boiled your vegetables—other**
>   **than potatoes—use that water)**

Remove the meat from the roasting pan; scoop off the fatty layer from the meat juices and discard. Then scrape the bottom of the pan to loosen all the caramelized bits and put the pan on the stove top.

Over low heat, add a little flour and stir it into the meat juices. Keep adding small amounts of flour until you get a thick paste. Keep cooking and stirring for 2 to 3 minutes until the mixture turns brown.

Add up to ½ cup stock, a little at a time, blending it with the paste as you go.

Keep the mixture just about at boiling point, and keep stirring as it thickens. When it has finished thickening, add more stock until you get the consistency you want. Continue cooking for another 1 to 2 minutes, then serve.

> **Tip:** *If you have roasted vegetables separately, include the juices and caramelized bits from that pan, too.*

MAINS: POULTRY

Chicken is an easy meat to prepare for babies and even those just starting out can usually eat it successfully, in strips or on the bone. Breast meat can be a little dry, so recipes that keep the meat moist are ideal at first. Most babies enjoy chicken drumsticks—but remember to remove gristle and splint bones first.

Lemon and Tarragon Chicken

This light chicken dish will give your baby the chance to discover the distinctive flavor of tarragon. It's a good dish for beginners because the chicken strips are easy to pick up.

Serves 2 adults and 1 baby

2 or 3 chicken breasts, cut into strips
2 tablespoons fresh lemon juice
1 tablespoon chopped fresh tarragon (or 1 teaspoon dried)
2 tablespoons heavy cream
Freshly ground black pepper, to taste

Put the chicken and lemon juice in a saucepan and heat until the juice is just boiling, then turn down the heat, cover, and simmer gently for about 10 minutes until the chicken is cooked. Add a little water, if necessary, to prevent the pan from scorching.

Add the tarragon, cream, and black pepper, and stir until the cream is warmed through.

Serve warm with rice, pasta, or couscous, and steamed vegetables.

Green Thai Curried Chicken and Rice

This is a quick and easy recipe to make. Chicken breast strips are good for a baby who is just beginning BLW to chomp on, and the peas are great fun for babies practicing their pincer grip.

This recipe uses a mild, homemade Thai green curry paste. If you use store-bought paste (which is likely to be hotter), reduce the amount stated in this recipe and taste the finished dish before offering it to your baby.

Serves 2 adults and 1 baby

Approx. 2 tablespoons Mild Thai Green Curry Paste (see page 180), to taste

2 or 3 chicken breasts, sliced to suit your baby

One 14-ounce can unsweetened coconut milk

¾ cup rice

1 or 2 handfuls frozen peas and/or green beans

Heat a large saucepan or wok on the stove top and add the Thai curry paste.

Add the chicken and fry briefly, until the outside of the chicken pieces is sealed. Add the coconut milk, bring to a boil, then reduce the heat and simmer for about 15 minutes.

Meanwhile, start cooking the rice (following the package instructions) so that it will be almost ready as the vegetables are becoming soft (the exact time needed will depend on the type of rice you use—but don't overcook it).

Add the frozen peas or beans to the curry and cook for a further 4 or 5 minutes (beans may need a little longer—about 6 minutes).

Add the rice to the chicken and vegetables and stir. Cook for a further 2 or 3 minutes to allow the rice to absorb some of the sauce.

Serve warm, on its own or with a salad.

Options

- A sliced red or yellow bell pepper will give added color and flavor.
- The green beans can be broken into smaller pieces if your baby can manage them.
- You may prefer to replace the rice with noodles.

Tomato Chicken

This is a delicious, warmly spiced dish that a baby starting out will be able to manage easily. It also works well with chicken thighs or drumsticks but may take longer to cook.

Serves 2 adults and 1 baby

Oil for frying
1 medium onion, chopped or cut into wedges
1 teaspoon ground cumin
2 teaspoons ground coriander
2 or 3 chicken breasts, cut into strips
One 14-ounce can tomatoes, chopped
1 tablespoon tomato paste
1 tablespoon chopped fresh cilantro (optional)

Heat the oil in a saucepan, add the onion, and fry for a few minutes until soft.

Add the cumin and coriander and cook for 2 or 3 minutes, then add the chicken and cook until lightly browned on all sides (but not cooked through).

Add the tomatoes and tomato paste. Bring to a boil, cover, and simmer for about 20 minutes, until the chicken is thoroughly cooked.

Sprinkle with the fresh cilantro before serving, warm, with rice and vegetables of your choice.

Option

- Try adding a little chili powder if you and your baby like spicy food.

Moroccan Chicken

This is a tasty introduction to Moroccan flavors. Babies just starting out will be able to manage the zucchini and chicken; older babies will be able to get hold of the chickpeas, too.

Serves 2 adults and 1 baby

Oil for frying

1 medium onion, finely chopped

1 or 2 teaspoons ground cumin

½ teaspoon ground cinnamon

3 chicken thighs

1¼ cups chicken or vegetable stock (low-sodium or homemade—see pages 176–177)

Pinch of chili powder (or more depending on your preference)

1 or 2 tablespoons roughly chopped fresh cilantro

1 large zucchini, cut into sticks

One 15-ounce can chickpeas, rinsed and drained

1 or 2 tablespoons chopped fresh parsley

Juice of 1 lemon (approx. 4 tablespoons)

Freshly ground black pepper, to taste

Heat the oil in a saucepan, add the onion, and fry for a few minutes until soft.

Add the cumin and cinnamon and cook for 2 or 3 minutes. Add the chicken thighs, stock, chili, and cilantro, and bring to a boil. Cover and simmer for 25 minutes.

Add the zucchini and chickpeas, bring back to a boil, and simmer for a further 10 to 20 minutes, until the zucchini is soft.

Stir in the parsley and the lemon juice. Add black pepper to taste and serve warm with couscous, rice, or quinoa. Cut the chicken into strips for your baby.

Option

• If you prefer a sweeter dish, and your baby is over a year old, you can add 1 tablespoon of clear honey with the oil, herbs, and spices.

Turkey and Vegetable Burgers

These burgers are good warm or cold, with homemade Spicy Tomato Salsa (see page 148). If you have time, put the burgers in the fridge to firm up for an hour or so before you cook them.

Serves 2 adults and 1 baby, generously

1 small parsnip, chopped

½ medium leek, finely chopped

9 ounces ground turkey

2 teaspoons fresh sage, chopped (or 1 teaspoon dried)

1 teaspoon dried mixed herbs

Freshly ground black pepper, to taste

Preheat the oven to 425°F and lightly grease a baking sheet.

Steam, boil, or microwave the parsnip and leek, then drain. Blend or mash thoroughly, to make a purée. Add the turkey and mix well. Add the herbs and black pepper and stir thoroughly.

Shape the mixture into about 8 burgers approx. ½-inch thick (flouring or wetting your hands will help to keep it from sticking), pressing them together and making sure they are all roughly the same thickness.

Bake in the oven for about 25 minutes until cooked through (remove one and test it by cutting it in half—there should be no pink meat).

Serve warm, with new potatoes or couscous, and vegetables.

Options

- If you prefer, you can cook the burgers in a frying pan, turning them once so that they brown on both sides. They also work well shaped into sausages.
- You can make similar burgers using pork instead of turkey and replacing the parsnip with 1 small apple (peeled, cored, and chopped) and 2 sticks of celery (chopped).

Chicken Stir-Fry with Noodles

This stir-fry is colorful, and the shapes are fun for small hands to grasp. Cut the vegetables very thin so they are not too crunchy for your baby.

Serves 2 adults and 1 baby

Approx. 4 ounces thin noodles, such as rice vermicelli
2 tablespoons oil
Approx. 2 teaspoons light sesame oil
2 medium carrots, peeled and cut into thin strips
4 whole baby corn, quartered lengthwise
1 red bell pepper, deseeded and cut into thin strips
1 yellow bell pepper, deseeded and cut into thin strips
1 garlic clove, finely chopped or crushed
1 celery stalk, strings removed, cut into very thin strips
2 chicken breasts, cut into strips

Cook the noodles according to the package instructions, then drain and return to the pan. Add a little of the oil and toss the noodles in it, then cover and set aside.

Heat a wok or a deep, nonstick frying pan and add a little sesame oil. Stir-fry the carrots, baby corn, and bell peppers for 30 seconds.

Add the garlic and celery and stir-fry for a further 30 seconds, then lift the vegetables out of the pan (draining off the oil) and set aside.

Heat some more of the sesame oil in the pan, if necessary, then add the chicken strips. Stir-fry for about 3 minutes, until the chicken is cooked through. Add the cooked vegetables and noodles and stir-fry for 1 minute.

Serve warm with, for the adults, a dash of soy sauce or tamari.

Options

• You can also add mushrooms, scallions, bok choy, finely sliced broccoli or green beans, snow peas or snap peas, or fresh sliced ginger to this dish. Toasted sesame seeds can be added just before serving; cashew nuts are also tasty, for children over five and adults.

• You can leave out the noodles and serve the stir-fry with rice instead.

MAINS: FISH

Fish is simple to prepare, quick to cook, and very nutritious. It can be grilled, fried, oven-baked, or stir-fried or made into fishcakes or fish pie, and the texture is easy for babies to eat. Just watch out for any bones, even if the fish has already been filleted.

Broiled Salmon

This is proper "fast" food—a simple, nutritious dish that takes just 10 minutes to cook. If you serve it with couscous and salad you can have the whole thing on the table in less than 15 minutes. Most fatty fish, including mackerel or bluefish, can be cooked this way.

Serves 2 adults and 1 baby

2 salmon fillets
Oil or butter (preferably unsalted)

Adjust an oven rack 4 to 6 inches from the broiler element and preheat the broiler. Put the salmon fillets on a baking sheet and brush salmon with the oil or butter. Broil for about 10 minutes, or until cooked through.

Serve warm, with rice, couscous, new or mashed potatoes, and vegetables or salad and a squeeze of lemon. Spicy Tomato Salsa (see page 148) is also good with broiled fish. Check carefully to make sure there are no bones in your baby's portion.

Fish 'n' Chips

This simple dish is a tasty way for your baby to try white fish, and the potato wedges are a healthier option than fries.

Serves 2 adults and 1 baby

1 pound potatoes (2 or 3 large potatoes)
Oil for greasing and coating the potatoes
2 large cod fillets (or other white fish)
1 egg
½ cup to 1 cup breadcrumbs (preferably stale or dried)
Freshly ground black pepper, to taste
Oil for frying

Cut the potatoes into wedges (skins on) or thick slices and put into a pan of cold water. Preheat the oven to 375°F.

Put enough oil into a small roasting pan to just cover the bottom and heat it (on the stove top is fine).

Dry the wedges with a clean dish towel, add to the hot oil and shake the pan to coat them. Put the pan in the oven and bake for about 20 minutes.

Meanwhile, pat the fish on both sides with paper towels to dry it.

Beat the egg in a shallow dish and put the breadcrumbs into another one, with a little black pepper.

Dip each fillet into the beaten egg so it is covered on all sides, then press it into the breadcrumbs on both sides, so that it is evenly coated.

Heat the oil in a frying pan and add the fish. Fry gently for about 5 minutes on each side, until the fish is cooked through and the coating is brown and crispy.

Serve the fish with a squeeze of lemon juice, with the potato wedges and some vegetables alongside. Check carefully to make sure there are no bones in your baby's portion.

Option

• You can use sweet potatoes instead of, or as well as, ordinary potatoes.

Baked Salmon and Pesto Parcels

Salmon is an easy fish for babies to eat, as it holds together well when cooked.

Serves 2 adults and 1 baby

2 salmon fillets
1 tablespoon fresh pesto (see page 178)

Preheat the oven to 375°F. Place each salmon fillet in the center of a piece of lightly greased aluminum foil (large enough to seal by crimping together). Spread the pesto over the fish. Close the foil over the top of each fillet and crimp together to make a loose parcel.

Place the wrapped fillets on a baking sheet and put them in the oven.

Bake for about 15 minutes, or until the fish is cooked through.

Serve warm, with rice or new potatoes and steamed vegetables or salad. Check carefully to make sure there are no bones in your baby's portion.

Options

- The same method can be used to make lemon and herb fish parcels. Just swap the pesto for a little butter, a squeeze of lemon juice, and some chopped dill, parsley, or basil.
- If you find the foil parcels too fussy (or you don't have any foil), you can cook the fillets together in a covered ovenproof dish.

Salmon and Broccoli Bake

This comforting baked dish is nicely balanced in terms of nutrition; with fish, vegetables, pasta, herbs and dairy foods. For a quicker way to make the sauce, see page 182.

Serves 2 adults and 1 baby, generously

9 ounces ziti (or other tubular or spiral pasta shapes)
1 medium head broccoli, cut into large florets
2 tablespoons butter (preferably unsalted)
2 tablespoons all-purpose flour
2 cups milk
2 tablespoons chopped fresh parsley (optional)
1 tablespoon chopped fresh dill (optional)
3 skinless salmon fillets, cut into large chunks
½ cup cheese, grated (or enough for topping)
¾ cup breadcrumbs, stale or dried (optional)

Cook the pasta in a pan of boiling water for slightly less than the time indicated on the package (so that it's "al dente"), then drain.

Steam or boil the broccoli until it is just starting to soften, then drain.

Preheat the oven to 350°F. To make the sauce, melt the butter in a pan and stir in the flour. Cook gently until the mixture starts to bubble. Remove the pan from the heat and gradually add the milk, stirring constantly. Return the pan to the heat and bring to a boil, still stirring. Simmer until thickened, stirring all the time. Stir in the parsley and dill.

Arrange the salmon chunks in a baking dish and add the pasta and broccoli. Pour on the sauce. Mix the cheese with the breadcrumbs, then sprinkle over the surface. Bake in the oven for 30 minutes.

Serve warm with vegetables—steamed baby carrots and green beans or asparagus go particularly well with this dish. Check carefully to make sure there are no bones in your baby's portion.

Fish Cakes

Fish cakes are easy for babies to grab and eat, even when they're just starting out.

Serves 2 adults and 1 baby

A little milk (or water) for poaching

8 ounces white fish or salmon fillets

8 ounces cooked potatoes (without skins)

2 tablespoons butter (preferably unsalted) for mashing potatoes (optional)

1 tablespoon chopped fresh cilantro or parsley

Zest of 1 unwaxed lemon (optional)

Freshly ground black pepper, to taste

¼ cup to ½ cup breadcrumbs, stale or dried

Oil for frying

Pour some milk into a shallow pan (with a lid), to a depth of about ¼ inch, and add the fish. Heat until the milk is just beginning to boil, then turn the heat down, cover, and simmer for about 5 minutes, until the fish is opaque and cooked in the center. Drain the fish thoroughly, then skin and flake it, removing any bones.

Mash the potatoes with the butter, herbs, lemon zest, and black pepper. Stir in the flaked fish with a little of the beaten egg.

Put the remainder of the egg in a shallow dish and put the breadcrumbs into another one. Flour your hands, then take small amounts of the mixture and shape into 4 or 5 fishcakes. Dip each fishcake into the beaten egg so it is covered on all sides, then roll it in the breadcrumbs, so that it is evenly coated.

Heat the oil in a large frying pan and add the fishcakes. Cook for about 5 minutes on each side, until golden brown. Serve warm, with roasted sweet potato wedges, steamed peas and corn or baked beans, or with a salad.

Option

• Canned salmon or tuna (in spring water or oil) can be used in place of fresh fish. A few chopped scallions added to the mixture is delicious.

Fish Sticks

These fish sticks can be made into exactly the right size and shape for your baby, and the coating is softer and less crunchy than a traditional breadcrumb coating. Perfect for BLW beginners.

"Chloe really loved homemade fish fingers, even when she was just starting out. They are the perfect shape for babies—really easy to eat and tasty."
—Jo-Ellen, mother of Chloe, 17 months

Serves 2 adults and 1 baby

10 ounces white fish fillet, (e.g., pollack, cod, or haddock)
1 egg
½ cup all-purpose flour
½ cup coarsely ground cornmeal
Oil or butter (preferably unsalted) for frying

Slice the fish into chunky fingers, making sure there are no bones.

Beat the egg in a shallow dish and mix together the flour and cornmeal in another dish. Dip each fish finger into the beaten egg so it is covered on all sides, then roll it in the flour and cornmeal mix so that it is evenly coated.

Heat the oil or butter in a frying pan. Fry the fish fingers in the hot oil or butter, turning as necessary, until they are brown and crispy on at least two sides.

Serve warm, with new potatoes and steamed vegetables or a salad.

Fish Pie

Although fish pie won't be an easy food for your baby to eat when he first starts out, he'll soon be able to manage it. Until then he'll have fun licking it off his fingers.

Serves 2 adults and 1 baby

1 pound starchy potatoes

10 ounces white fish fillet (pollack, cod, haddock)

¾ cup milk

1½ tablespoons butter (preferably unsalted)

1½ tablespoons all-purpose flour

1 tablespoon chopped fresh parsley (optional)

Pinch of freshly ground black pepper (optional)

½ cup grated cheese

Bring the potatoes to a boil. Simmer the fish in a saucepan with ½ cup of the milk for about 10 minutes until opaque, then lift out with a slotted spoon, reserving the milk. Break the fish up into flakes—discarding any skin and bones—and set aside.

When the potatoes are soft (about 25 minutes), drain and mash them with about 1½ tablespoons of the uncooked milk and 1 teaspoon of the butter, until smooth and creamy.

Preheat the oven to 400°F. To make the sauce, melt the remaining butter in a pan and stir in the flour. Cook gently until the mixture starts to bubble. Remove the pan from the heat and gradually add the milk used for poaching the fish, followed by the remainder of the milk, stirring constantly to prevent lumps from forming. Return the pan to the heat and bring to a boil, still stirring. Reduce the heat and simmer until thickened, stirring all the time.

Remove the sauce from the heat and stir in the flaked fish, parsley, and black pepper (if using). Pour the mixture into an ovenproof dish, spread the mashed potatoes on top, then cover with the grated cheese.

Oven bake for 20 to 30 minutes, until the surface is golden. Serve warm with a selection of vegetables or a salad.

Option

• Try adding some precooked leeks, green beans, or corn to the fish mixture, or mash some cooked rutabaga, parsnip, or carrot with the potato.

Smoked Mackerel Pasta

This delicious, simple dish is perfect for a baby who is learning to pick up slippery things but still needs some stick shapes that he can grip easily. If you break the mackerel into fairly big chunks, he'll be able to get hold of them, too. Smoked mackerel is quite salty, so don't give your baby too much of it.

Serves 2 adults and 1 baby

4 to 6 small broccoli florets

4 to 6 string beans, with "strings" removed and sliced to suit your baby

2 or 3 fillets of smoked mackerel, skinned

Oil or butter (preferably unsalted) for frying

1 garlic clove, sliced or chopped

1 teaspoon chopped fresh oregano

6 to 8 fresh basil leaves

2 to 2½ tablespoons butter (preferably unsalted)

8 ounces rotini (or other tubular or spiral pasta shapes)

½ cup to 1 cup Parmesan cheese, grated (optional)

Steam or boil the broccoli and string beans until tender, then drain.

Break the mackerel into chunks, making sure there are no bones.

Heat the oil or butter in a frying pan, add the garlic, and fry gently for 1 or 2 minutes. Remove the pan from the heat, lift out the garlic and set aside. While off the heat, add the oregano and basil to the pan, and stir in the butter. Add the steamed broccoli, beans, and mackerel, and stir well. Return the pan to low heat, add the garlic, and warm the mixture through gently.

Cook the pasta in a large saucepan of boiling water according to the instructions on the packet until just soft, then drain. Divide the pasta among individual plates with the fish mixture on top, and sprinkle with Parmesan cheese (if using), to taste.

Serve warm on its own or with a side salad.

Thai Green Fish Curry

Although Thai curries can be fairly hot, if you use our Mild Thai Green Curry Paste (see page 180), this will be a good curry for your baby to try. If you make it with store-bought curry paste, reduce the amount stated in this recipe and taste the finished dish before offering it to your baby for the first time.

Serves 2 adults and 1 baby

1 pound thick white fish fillets (e.g. cod, haddock, monkfish)

Oil for frying

1 or 2 garlic cloves, finely chopped or crushed (optional)

One 14-ounce can unsweetened coconut milk

1 or 2 tablespoons Mild Thai Green Curry Paste (see page 180), to taste

4 to 6 green beans, trimmed

4 kaffir lime leaves or 2 slices of fresh lime

3 or 4 cherry tomatoes (optional)

4 or 5 fresh cilantro leaves, chopped

6 to 8 fresh basil leaves, chopped

Cut the fish into thick chunks or short fingers to suit your baby, making sure there are no bones.

Heat the oil in a frying pan and add the garlic. Fry gently for a minute or two.

Add the coconut milk to the pan (take care—it may splash). Bring to a boil very gently, stirring constantly, then add the curry paste. Simmer gently and add the fish, green beans, and lime leaves/slices.

Simmer gently for 9 or 10 minutes, then add the tomatoes (if using) and cook for a further 2 or 3 minutes, until the fish is cooked.

Sprinkle with cilantro and basil and serve with plain or sticky rice.

MAINS: EGGS & CHEESE

Eggs and cheese are versatile and nutritious and, because they keep well, they make good "pantry" meals. However, cheese is quite salty, so be sure to serve with plenty of vegetables.

Potato, Leek, and Cheese Bake

This simple dish is easy to make and very tasty. See page 182 for an alternative way to make the sauce.

Serves 2 adults and 1 baby

1 pound potatoes (2 or 3 large potatoes), cut into fairly thick slices

Oil or butter (preferably unsalted) for frying

1 medium leek, washed and cut into chunks

2 tablespoons butter (preferably unsalted)

2½ tablespoons all-purpose flour

1 cup milk

½ cup to ¾ cup grated cheese

Steam or boil the potatoes until just cooked and allow to cool.

Heat the oil or butter in a saucepan, add the leek, and fry gently until soft.

Preheat the oven to 350°F. Melt the 2 tablespoons of butter in a pan and stir in the flour. Cook gently for 2 or 3 minutes until the mixture starts to bubble. Remove the pan from the heat and gradually add the milk, stirring constantly. Return the pan to the heat and bring to a boil, still stirring. Keep stirring the sauce at boiling point until thickened. Remove from the heat and stir in almost all the cheese.

Layer the potatoes over the bottom of an ovenproof dish. Spread the leek on top and pour on the cheese sauce. Sprinkle the remaining cheese on top.

Bake for about 20 minutes, until the surface is golden.

Homity Pie

This potato and onion pie is delicious; serve it with sticks of vegetables if your baby is just starting out.

Makes 1 large pie or 6 individual pies

1 recipe Simple Pastry Dough (see page 175), or 1 prebaked single pie crust (or, for individual pies, 11 ounces pastry dough—about 1½ of the Simple Pastry Dough recipe)

Approx. 12 ounces potatoes

Oil or butter (preferably unsalted) for frying

1 pound onions, chopped

2 tablespoons butter (preferably unsalted)

1 to 2 garlic cloves, finely chopped or crushed

2 teaspoons chopped fresh parsley

Pinch of dried thyme

Pinch of freshly ground black pepper

1 tablespoon milk

¾ cup grated cheese

To prepare your pie crust either line a 9-inch pie pan (or six 4-inch pans) with pastry dough (and bake "blind" if you like—see page 175) or use a store-bought prebaked pie crust.

Steam or boil the potatoes until just cooked and allow to cool (or use previously boiled potatoes).

Preheat the oven to 425°F. Heat the oil or butter in a pan, add the onions, and fry gently until soft.

Meanwhile, slice or chop the potatoes and put them into a large bowl. Add the onions, butter, garlic, herbs, black pepper, milk, and half the cheese, and mix well.

Transfer the mixed ingredients to the lined pie pan and sprinkle the remaining cheese on top. Bake for 20 to 25 minutes until golden brown.

Serve warm, with a selection of vegetables.

Options
• Try replacing three-quarters of the onions with leeks, washed and cut into chunks.
• Mix some breadcrumbs with the cheese sprinkled on top, for a slightly crunchy crust.

Simple Broccoli Quiche

This tasty quiche is traditionally made with Gruyère cheese, but Cheddar works, too.

Makes 1 large quiche or 6 individual quiches

1 medium head broccoli (florets only)

1 recipe Simple Pastry Dough (see page 175), or 1 prebaked single pie crust (or, for individual pies, 11 ounces pastry dough—about 1½ of the Simple Pastry Dough recipe)

1 small onion, finely sliced

¾ cup grated cheese (according to taste)

3 eggs

½ cup milk

Pinch of freshly ground black pepper

> **Storage:** *Quiches are easy to cook in batches, for freezing. They can be kept for 2 to 3 days in the fridge.*

Preheat the oven to 375°F. Cut the broccoli into small florets and steam or boil for about 2 minutes until just tender, then drain.

To prepare your pie crust, either line a 9-inch pie pan (or six 4-inch pans) with dough (and "blind" bake if you like—see page 175) or use a store-bought prebaked pie crust. Spread the onion in the bottom of the lined pie pan, add the broccoli, and sprinkle half of the cheese over it.

Beat together the eggs and milk and add the black pepper. Pour the egg mixture over the onion, broccoli, and cheese, then sprinkle the remaining cheese on top. (The egg mixture should come at least three-quarters of the way up the pastry case. If it doesn't, add another egg, beaten with about 2 tablespoons milk.)

Bake in the oven for 40 to 50 minutes, until the egg is cooked through (test it with a skewer) and the crust is golden brown.

Serve warm, sliced, or in fingers, with new potatoes and either salad, green beans, or asparagus for a main meal, or eat it cold for a light lunch.

Options

• Alternative fillings include: a few slices of cooked bacon, chopped; a little ham, cut into strips; sliced tomatoes, or halved cherry tomatoes; sliced mushrooms; shredded spinach; chopped asparagus.

• For a really rich quiche, replace some of the milk with half-and-half.

• For a more cheesy quiche, use cheese-flavored pie crust (see options, page 175).

Lentil Quiche

This makes a heartier than usual quiche that is rich in nutrients and very tasty. Serve it in small slices or "fingers" for your baby.

Makes 1 large quiche or 6 individual quiches

Oil or butter (preferably unsalted) for frying

1 garlic clove, finely chopped or crushed

1 medium leek, finely chopped

¾ cup red lentils, rinsed in cold water and drained

2 cups milk

Pinch of dried thyme

1 recipe Simple Pastry Dough (see page 175), or 1 prebaked single pie crust (or, for individual pies, 11 ounces pastry dough—about 1½ of the Simple Pastry Dough recipe)

2 eggs

¾ cup cheese, grated

3 medium tomatoes, sliced

Heat the oil or butter in a pan, add the garlic and leek, and fry until soft.

Add the lentils and stir. Add the milk and thyme and bring to a boil.

Reduce the heat, cover, and simmer gently for 30 to 40 minutes, checking and stirring every 5 minutes until the lentils are soft and the mixture is nice and thick. Remove from the heat and set aside.

While the lentils are cooking, prepare your pie crust: either line a 9-inch pie pan (or six 4-inch pans) with pie dough (you can "blind" bake this if you like—see page 175) or use a store-bought crust.

Preheat the oven to 375°F. In a bowl, beat the eggs and stir in half the cheese. Add the cheese and eggs to the lentil mixture and stir to mix.

Pour the mixture into the lined pie pan. Sprinkle with the remaining cheese and place the tomato slices on top.

Bake in the oven for about 45 minutes, until the egg is cooked through (test with a skewer) and the surface is golden brown.

Serve warm or cold, with new potatoes and vegetables or a salad.

Frittata

Frittata is a lovely recipe, and the fillings can be varied so it's different every time. It can be made with freshly cooked vegetables but is also a great way to use up any leftovers.

Serves 2 adults and 1 baby

2 large potatoes (14 ounces)
4 eggs
1 tablespoon milk
2 teaspoons chopped fresh parsley
Pinch of freshly ground black pepper (optional)
Oil for frying
1 medium onion, chopped
1 or 2 garlic cloves, chopped
Filling of your choice (see options, below)

Steam or boil the potatoes until soft and allow to cool (or use previously boiled potatoes). Slice thinly and set aside.

Beat the eggs and milk together and stir in the parsley and black pepper.

Heat the oil in an 8-inch frying pan with an ovenproof handle. Add the onion, and fry gently until soft. Add the garlic and cook for another minute or two, then add the potatoes and heat through, moving them around so that they don't stick.

Pour the egg mixture over the other ingredients in the frying pan. Stir once, quickly, to ensure they are all coated. Cook until the egg is thoroughly set (test by inserting a skewer—it should come out clean). Meanwhile, preheat the broiler.

Put the pan under the broiler for 3 to 5 minutes until the frittata begins to brown on top.

Serve warm or cold, on its own or with vegetables or a salad.

Options

• The beauty of this recipe is that you can put almost any sautéed or precooked vegetables or meat you want into it. Try chopped ham or bacon, bell pepper (green, red, yellow or orange), eggplant, peas or green beans, mushrooms, broccoli or cauliflower, tomatoes, zucchini, or butternut squash.
• Try sprinkling grated cheese on top of the frittata before you put it under the broiler.

MAINS: VEGETABLE-BASED

There are plenty of textures and tastes for your baby to try out in our selection of healthy vegetable-based dishes.

Ratatouille

This dish is ideal for BLW beginners, as the vegetables can be cut into chunky sticks.

Serves 2 adults and 1 baby

Oil for frying

1 large onion, sliced into thin rings

1 large eggplant, cut to suit your baby

1 bell pepper, preferably red, cut to suit your baby

2 zucchinis, cut to suit your baby

2 or 3 garlic cloves, finely chopped or crushed

3 or 4 large ripe tomatoes (or a 14-ounce can of plum tomatoes)

1 teaspoon dried oregano

Pinch of freshly ground black pepper

1 tablespoon tomato paste (optional)

Heat the oil in a frying pan and fry the onion for a few minutes. Add the eggplant, bell pepper, zucchini, and garlic and cook for 5 to 10 minutes, turning occasionally, until soft.

Meanwhile, blanch the tomatoes (if using fresh) in boiling water until the skins begin to split, then drain, immerse in cold water, remove the skins, and roughly chop.

Add the oregano, black pepper, and tomatoes to the pan, and stir well.

Continue to cook on low heat for 20 to 30 minutes, until the tomatoes have made a thick sauce. Serve warm, with rice or pasta, as an accompaniment to a main dish such as quiche, or on its own with chunks of fresh bread and butter.

Tofu and Bell Pepper Stir-Fry

Stir-fried tofu is usually marinated with soy sauce or tamari, but, as these are too salty for babies, this recipe uses ginger and sesame oil, which give a lovely fresh flavor. Adults may like to add tamari or soy sauce to their own portion.

Serves 2 adults and 1 baby

6 ounces firm tofu (not silken), cut into chunks to suit your baby

1-inch piece of fresh ginger, peeled and finely sliced

3 tablespoons light sesame oil

2 bell peppers (red, yellow, or orange), thinly sliced lengthwise

4 scallions, roughly chopped

6 to 8 cherry or grape tomatoes

Put the tofu into a bowl with the ginger and 2 tablespoons of the sesame oil, and leave it to marinate for 15 minutes.

Heat a wok or a deep, nonstick frying pan until very hot and add the rest of the sesame oil.

Add the ginger from the marinade and cook for 30 seconds or so. Add the bell peppers, scallions, and tomatoes and stir-fry for 5 to 10 minutes until tender, keeping the pan hot and stirring/tossing everything constantly.

Add the tofu (discarding the marinade) and stir-fry for about 2 minutes.

Serve warm with noodles or basmati or sticky rice. Halve the tomatoes in your baby's portion.

Option

- Adults may enjoy a handful of toasted sesame seeds, peanuts or cashew nuts added just before serving, together with a dash of soy sauce or tamari.

Mild Lentil and Vegetable Curry

This is a lightly spiced curry that will introduce your baby to a range of flavors and textures—and there are plenty of shapes that he'll be able to get hold of easily if he's just starting out. If you can't find okra, you can use green beans instead.

Serves 2 adults and 1 baby

1 or 2 tablespoons oil

2 medium red onions, finely chopped

2 cardamom pods

½-inch piece of fresh ginger, peeled and finely chopped

Approx. 2 tablespoons Quick Curry Paste (see page 179)

1 bay leaf

2 new potatoes, skins on and halved or quartered, depending on size

3 broccoli florets, cut to suit your baby

3 cauliflower florets, cut to suit your baby

1 medium carrot, cut to suit your baby

3 okras, topped and tailed, and cut into pieces to suit your baby

2 or 3 tablespoons frozen peas

1 small zucchini, cut to suit your baby

½ cup red lentils, rinsed in cold water and drained

1½ cups coconut milk

Heat the oil in a large saucepan, add the onions, and fry gently for 10 minutes until they are golden. Meanwhile, split open the cardamom pods and remove the seeds (discard the pods). Add the seeds to the pan, with the ginger, curry paste, and bay leaf, and fry for a few minutes, stirring occasionally to prevent everything from sticking.

Add the potatoes, broccoli, cauliflower, carrot, and okra. Cook for a few minutes, stirring occasionally, to coat the vegetables in the spices.

Add the rest of the vegetables, together with the lentils and coconut milk.

Bring to a boil, cover, and simmer for 20 minutes until the lentils are tender and the vegetables are cooked, stirring occasionally to prevent the food from sticking and burning.

The liquid should now have reduced by half—simmer for a little longer with the lid off if you want a drier curry. Remove the bay leaf and serve warm, with rice, plain yogurt (or Yogurt and Cucumber Dip, see page 68), salad, and naan bread or chapatis (see page 161).

Saag Paneer or Tofu

This gentle curry is traditionally made with paneer, a mild white cheese that is especially useful when cooking for babies because it's unsalted. If you can't find paneer, the recipe works equally well with firm tofu (not "silken"). (Remember to wash your hands after handling the raw chili pepper, and before touching your baby, because chili juice can sting.)

Serves 2 adults and 1 baby

10 ounces spinach

Oil or butter (preferably unsalted) for frying

1 teaspoon cumin seeds

1 medium onion, sliced

2 garlic cloves, finely chopped or crushed

1-inch piece of fresh ginger, peeled and finely chopped

1 tablespoon garam masala

¼ mild fresh chili pepper (such as jalapeño), finely chopped (deseeded and veins removed), or a pinch of dried chili flakes

8 ounces paneer cheese (or firm tofu), chopped to suit your baby

2 tablespoons heavy cream

Lightly steam the spinach and blend it into a paste (a blender or food processor is best but a fork will do).

Heat the oil or butter in a large frying pan. Add the cumin seeds and fry for about 2 minutes until they start to become fragrant and make a popping sound. Add the onion, and fry until soft. Add the garlic, ginger, garam masala, and chili, and stir. Add the spinach paste, with a little water, if required, to make a runny sauce. Bring to a boil, then reduce the heat.

Add the paneer (or tofu) and cream and simmer for about 3 minutes.

Serve warm, with rice or naan bread.

Green Bean and Fennel Stir-Fry

This tasty stir-fry is light and fresh-tasting and has plenty of stick shapes and strips to get hold of—slice them finely until your baby can deal with crunchier textures.

This recipe uses Japanese rice vinegar, which is much milder than Western vinegars. Many large supermarkets stock it, but if you can't find it, you can use white wine vinegar diluted with water (three parts vinegar to one part water).

Serves 2 adults and 1 baby

1 ounce unsweetened shredded coconut

Warm water

4 ounces noodles

1 tablespoon oil for frying

1 garlic clove, finely chopped or crushed

4 scallions, chopped

½ fennel bulb, core removed and sliced finely

4 ounces haricot verts (French green beans), whole or sliced in half lengthwise (depending on how crunchy you want them)

4 ounces sugar or snap peas, whole or sliced to suit your baby

1 medium celery stick, sliced into very thin sticks

2 teaspoons rice vinegar

1 or 2 tablespoons chopped fresh cilantro or parsley

Put the coconut into a bowl of warm water, cover, and leave for 20 minutes. Meanwhile, cook the noodles according to the instructions on the package, then drain well and set aside. Strain the coconut through a sieve and set aside.

Heat a wok or deep nonstick frying pan until very hot, add the oil and then the garlic, onions, and fennel, and stir-fry for 2 minutes, keeping the pan very hot. Add the beans, peas, and celery, and stir-fry briefly. Add the rice vinegar, stir, then remove the pan from the heat. Sprinkle on the coconut, cilantro, or parsley, and stir.

Arrange the noodles in serving bowls with the stir-fried vegetables on top. Serve warm, with, for adults, a dash of tamari or soy sauce.

Bean and Vegetable Chili

"Grace really enjoys picking up the kidney beans in the vegetable chili with her fingers. She'll eat them first and then pick out other bits."

—Kim, mother of Grace, 11 months

Serves 2 adults and 1 baby

Oil for frying

1 medium onion, chopped

1 red bell pepper, deseeded and cut to suit your baby

1 medium zucchini, cut to suit your baby

1 teaspoon ground cumin

Pinch of chili powder or flakes, or to taste

1 teaspoon dried coriander, or 1 tablespoon chopped fresh cilantro

One 14-ounce can chopped tomatoes

One 15-ounce can red kidney beans, drained (or ½ cup dried beans, precooked—see page 45)

Heat the oil in a large saucepan and add the onion. Fry until soft. Add the bell pepper and zucchini, and cook until they begin to soften. Add the spices and herbs and cook for 1 minute, stirring constantly.

Add the tomatoes and beans and mix well. Bring to a boil, cover, and simmer for 15 to 20 minutes, until all the vegetables are soft.

Serve warm, with rice or couscous.

Options

• Any vegetables can be included in this chili. Try swapping the bell pepper and zucchini for some chopped mushrooms, squash, carrot, or sweet potato (which may need to be cooked for a little longer). Chopped spinach can be added when the rest of the vegetables are soft, and cooked for just a few minutes.

• You can replace the red kidney beans with similar beans, such as cannellini or pinto. If using dried beans, they will need to be presoaked and possibly precooked (see page 45).

MAINS: PIZZA, PASTA & RICE

Meals based on pizza, pasta, or rice are usually a big hit with everyone in the family—and they generally contain a variety of shapes that babies will enjoy.

Homemade Pizza

Frozen and take-out pizzas are almost always high in salt, so making your own is a healthy option and means that you can confidently share the meal with your baby. Older children and toddlers usually love creating their own pizzas from scratch. Make your own dough (or use store-bought), add a thick tomato sauce, some cheese (traditionally mozzarella, although other cheeses, such as Cheddar, can be used) and your favorite toppings.

Makes 1 pizza, enough for 2 adults and 1 baby

For the dough:
3 tablespoons olive oil, plus extra for greasing
1¾ cups all-purpose flour, plus extra for dusting
2½ teaspoons baking powder
Pinch of salt (optional)
½ cup warm water, plus more as needed
Toppings of your choice (see page 128)
For the sauce:
Oil for frying
1 garlic clove, finely chopped or crushed
One 14-ounce can crushed tomatoes
2 tablespoons tomato paste
1 teaspoon dried oregano
Pinch of freshly ground black pepper

Lightly grease a pizza pan or large baking sheet. Put the flour and baking powder into a bowl (with the salt, if using), and make a well in the center. Pour in the oil and most of the water. Mix until you have an elastic (but not sticky) dough, adding more water as necessary.

Transfer the dough to a floured surface and knead until it is an even color and feels uniformly elastic. Roll out the dough, shaping it into a round or oblong to fit your pan.

To make the sauce, heat the oil in a saucepan and fry the garlic for a minute or so. Add the remaining ingredients and simmer uncovered, so that the liquid reduces, for about 10 minutes, until the sauce is thick enough to cling to the pizza dough.

Preheat the oven to 425°F. Spread a generous layer of thick tomato sauce over the pizza base. Sprinkle with grated cheese and add any additional toppings, including a final layer of cheese, if you like.

Put the pizza in the oven and bake for 10 to 20 minutes, until the top is bubbling in the middle.

Suggested Toppings

Almost anything can be used as a pizza topping, but here are some favorites:

- Chopped bacon, ham, or salami (not too much—these are very salty)
- Lean ground beef or shredded chicken
- Sliced tomatoes, or halved cherry tomatoes
- Sliced mushrooms
- Corn
- Sliced red, yellow, or green bell peppers
- Spinach, broccoli, or leek
- Sliced eggplant or zucchini
- Mozzarella cheese
- Olives (in olive oil, not brine)

Pasta

Pasta is the perfect quick and easy meal for busy families. Many sauces can easily be prepared beforehand and are ideal for batch cooking and freezing; if you are really in a hurry, simply serve it with a spoonful of pesto (see page 178 for a homemade version). Choose pasta shapes to suit your baby's dexterity.

Cooking Pasta

Pasta needs to move while cooking to keep it from sticking together, so it's best to cook it in a large pan with plenty of water, which is kept boiling vigorously. Although many traditionalists say it should be cooked in salted water, as long as you're careful not to overcook the pasta, the texture should be fine when cooked without salt, which is better for babies. Don't add oil while it's cooking—it will prevent any sauce from coating the pasta properly later, and make it more slippery for your baby to hold. For best results, follow the instructions on the package for the recommended cooking time—but take a piece out to test for texture a minute or so before the recommended time is up.

Simple Tomato Pasta Sauce

This simple sauce is ideal for serving with pasta and is easy to make in batches for freezing. It's delicious mixed with grilled or roasted zucchini, eggplant, and bell peppers, or as the basis for other sauces, such as Bolognese (see page 132). It can also be served with chicken and fish.

Makes about 12 ounces

2 tablespoons olive oil
1 medium onion, finely chopped
1 or 2 garlic cloves, finely chopped or crushed
One 14-ounce can chopped tomatoes
2 tablespoons tomato paste
A handful of fresh basil leaves, torn
Pinch of freshly ground black pepper
1 bay leaf

Heat the oil in a saucepan, add the onion, and fry gently until soft. Add the garlic and cook gently for another minute or two, then add the tomatoes. Stir in the tomato paste, basil, and black pepper, then add the bay leaf. Simmer gently for about 20 minutes. Remove the bay leaf, blend the sauce if you wish, then serve warm with pasta.

Options

- Try spicing this sauce up by adding a few dried chili flakes.
- Add some finely grated celery and carrot with the onion for extra flavor.
- Try using fresh plum or cherry tomatoes (chopped or halved) with the canned tomatoes.

Tuna and Tomato Pasta

This is a really simple, tasty, pantry pasta dish that can be prepared in no time.

Serves 2 adults and 1 baby

8 ounces rotini (or other tubular or spiral pasta shapes)
Oil for frying
1 medium red onion, finely chopped
One 5-ounce can tuna (low-sodium, in spring water or oil)
1 garlic clove, finely chopped or crushed
1 teaspoon dried mixed herbs/herbes de Provence
One 14-ounce can chopped tomatoes or one 14-ounce can of crushed tomatoes (or half of each)
Dash of balsamic vinegar, to taste

Cook the pasta in a large saucepan of boiling water according to the instructions on the package, then drain well.

Meanwhile, make the sauce. Heat the oil in a frying pan and fry the onion for a few minutes, until soft. Break up the tuna and add it to the pan along with the garlic. Cook for 2 or 3 minutes. Add the herbs and stir to mix. Add the tomatoes and the balsamic vinegar, and stir. Allow to simmer for about 5 minutes, or longer if you want a thicker sauce.

Pour the sauce over the pasta and serve with a side salad.

Macaroni and Cheese

This tasty favorite tends to be a bit salty, so don't offer it to your baby too often. You can add some vegetables to the sauce to make it a more balanced meal. For an alternative way to make the sauce, see page 182.

"Callum really enjoys macaroni and cheese. We always put broccoli, onions, and cauliflower in it. He carefully picks out the onions and then eats the rest."
—Helen, mother of Callum, 11 months

Serves 2 adults and 1 baby

8 ounces macaroni (or other tubular or spiral pasta shapes)

2 tablespoons butter (preferably unsalted)

2 tablespoons all-purpose flour

1⅓ cups milk

1 to 1½ cups cheese, grated (a mix of Parmesan and Cheddar is good)

A splash of Worcestershire sauce, to taste (optional)

Nutmeg, for grating, or ½ teaspoon ready-ground nutmeg (optional)

½ cup breadcrumbs, stale or dried (optional)

8 to 10 cherry tomatoes, halved (optional)

Preheat the oven to 400°F. Cook the pasta in a large saucepan of boiling water according to the instructions on the package, then drain well.

Meanwhile, make the sauce. Melt the butter in a frying pan and stir in the flour. Cook gently for 2 or 3 minutes until the mixture starts to bubble. Remove the pan from the heat and gradually add the milk, stirring constantly. Return the pan to the heat and bring to a boil, still stirring. Simmer until thickened, stirring all the time. Remove from the heat and stir in almost all of the cheese, with the Worcestershire sauce and a little nutmeg. Add the cooked pasta and stir well.

Pour the mixture into an ovenproof dish, then sprinkle with the remaining cheese and the breadcrumbs and arrange the cherry tomatoes on top (cut-side-up). Put into the oven and bake for 10 to 20 minutes, until the cheese is bubbly and beginning to turn brown.

Serve warm, with salad or vegetables.

131

Bolognese Sauce

Most babies love a meat sauce such as Bolognese, and as soon as they can they will pick up handfuls and push it into their mouths. If you leave some of the meat in clumps while you are frying it, your baby will find it easier to pick up. And if you plan to serve the sauce with spaghetti, have your camera ready—it can be fantastically messy! Many people say Bolognese sauce tastes better made several hours before you plan to eat it, then kept in the fridge so the flavors can mature (be sure to reheat it thoroughly before serving). If you are making the sauce for a lasagna (see page 134), add a little water during the cooking if necessary, to keep it runny.

Serves 2 adults and 1 baby

1 slice bacon, finely chopped (using scissors is easiest)

1 medium red onion, finely chopped

Oil for frying (if needed)

8 ounces lean ground beef

1 garlic clove, finely chopped or crushed (optional)

1 medium carrot, finely chopped or grated

1 celery stick, strings removed and finely chopped

2 ounces mushrooms, sliced

One 14-ounce can tomatoes, chopped

1 tablespoon tomato paste

1 or 2 teaspoons dried oregano or 1 tablespoon fresh oregano leaves

1 bay leaf

Small bunch of fresh basil leaves, torn

Freshly ground black pepper, to taste (optional)

¾ cup grated Parmesan cheese, to serve

Heat a large saucepan and add the bacon and onion. Fry until the onion is soft (the bacon will be fatty so you probably won't need any oil). Add the ground beef and cook for about 5 minutes until the meat is browned. Add the garlic and cook for another minute. Add the carrot, celery, mushrooms, tomatoes, tomato paste, and oregano, and mix well. Add the bay leaf, bring to a boil, cover, and simmer for 20 minutes. Check occasionally, and add a little water if the sauce appears too thick.

Just before serving, remove the bay leaf and add the torn basil leaves, along with some black pepper, if desired. Top with freshly grated or shaved Parmesan cheese.

Serve warm, with a pasta of your choice—either mixed in or poured over the top—on its own or with a green salad.

Options

- You can make a similar sauce with ground pork or a mixture of pork and beef.
- If you have some ready-made Simple Tomato Sauce (see page 129), just fry the meat, stir in the sauce and cook until it's thoroughly heated through.

> **Storage:** *Bolognese sauce freezes very well, so it's worth doubling or tripling the quantities so you have some on hand.*

Pasta with Asparagus

"We offered Tom asparagus and I think he thought it was a green bean—which he loves—but he looked really puzzled and disappointed. I don't think it was that he didn't like the asparagus—just that it wasn't what he was expecting."
—Liz, mother of Tom, 2 years

Serves 2 adults and 1 baby

8 ounces penne (or other tubular or spiral pasta shapes)

12 medium-sized whole asparagus spears

2 tablespoons butter (preferably unsalted)

2 garlic cloves, crushed

1 tablespoon chopped fresh basil

½ cup grated Parmesan cheese

Cook the pasta in a large saucepan of boiling water according to the instructions on the package, then drain well. Meanwhile trim the asparagus spears by chopping off any woody bits at the base of the stem. Steam the trimmed tips for 5 minutes, or until tender.

Melt the butter gently in a large frying pan. Add the garlic and cook gently for 30 seconds. Stir in the drained pasta and basil. Mix in the asparagus spears so they are coated in butter.

Sprinkle with Parmesan cheese and serve warm, with a green salad.

Options

- Green beans or broccoli can be used instead of asparagus.
- You can add one 5-ounce can of tuna (low-sodium, in oil) when you stir in the pasta.
- Try fresh parsley or sage in place of the basil.

133

Classic Lasagna

Many babies enjoy dismantling the layers of a lasagna and eating the different bits individually, but beginners may find it tricky to pick up, so it's a good idea to serve it alongside something easy to manage, such as broccoli.

The two main sauces in this lasagna (Bolognese and a béchamel or cheese sauce) lend themselves to batch cooking, so if you already have some made, this dish is fairly quick to prepare—especially if you buy lasagna noodles that don't need pre-boiling. If you are starting from scratch you will need to allow plenty of time. The size of your dish will determine how many layers deep your lasagna is. Choose a wide dish if you only want a couple of layers.

Make sure your sauces are fairly runny, because the lasagna noodles will absorb water from them. Just add a little water (to Bolognese sauce) or milk (to béchamel or cheese sauce) as necessary.

Serves 2 adults and 1 baby, very generously

1 batch of Bolognese sauce (page 132)

One package of quick-cooking lasagna noodles

2 or 3 batches of béchamel or cheese sauce (see page 182)

3 medium tomatoes, sliced (optional)

1 cup grated Parmesan cheese (optional—you may need less if you are using a cheese sauce)

Ground nutmeg

Preheat the oven to 375°F. Put a shallow layer of Bolognese sauce in the bottom of an ovenproof dish. Cover with a single layer of lasagna noodles, breaking them as necessary to minimize overlapping. Pour over a layer of béchamel/cheese sauce. Repeat these three layers up to three more times, depending on the width of your dish, making sure the last layer is béchamel/cheese sauce.

Arrange the tomato slices on top and sprinkle with Parmesan cheese and nutmeg. Put into the oven and bake for about 30 minutes, until browned on top.

Serve warm, cut into rough slices, with a simple green salad or some broccoli or green beans.

Portobello Mushroom Carbonara

Carbonara sauce is traditionally made with raw eggs, but this delicious version gets by without them. Slices of large portobello mushrooms will give your baby an easy shape to handle, but smaller mushrooms will taste just as good.

Serves 2 adults and 1 baby

8 ounces rotini (or other tubular or spiral pasta shapes)

4 tablespoons butter (preferably unsalted)

2 slices lean bacon, cut into small pieces

4 large portobello mushrooms, cut into thick slices

1 or 2 garlic cloves, finely chopped or crushed

1 cup half-and-half

1 tablespoon chopped fresh parsley or basil

½ cup grated Parmesan cheese

Cook the pasta in a large saucepan of boiling water according to the instructions on the package, then drain well.

Melt the butter gently in a large frying pan. Add the pieces of bacon and cook over low heat for 1 minute. Add the sliced mushrooms and garlic and cook for another 2 minutes. Stir in the half-and-half and parsley or basil, and continue cooking gently for a further 3 or 4 minutes, stirring occasionally.

Pour the sauce over the pasta and sprinkle with Parmesan cheese.

Serve warm, with a green salad.

Rice

Rice is great for helping babies to develop their self-feeding skills, but there's no need to aim for "perfect" light, fluffy rice when your baby is just starting out; most babies do better with rice that they can pick up in clumps, such as Thai sticky rice, Japanese sushi rice, or risotto rice. If long-grain rice is all you have in the house, just overcook it slightly, so that it sticks together. Later, once your baby starts using a pincer grip, he'll enjoy picking up individual grains.

As a general rule, rice needs to absorb roughly its own volume of water (that is, a cup of rice will absorb a cup of water), although more needs to be added to allow for water lost as steam. However, cooking rice in too much water makes it sticky—as does boiling it too rapidly and stirring it while it's cooking. Basmati rice is traditionally presoaked to keep the grains separate when cooked (it's then fluffed up with a fork before serving). In general, when cooking rice, follow the package instructions for the best results.

"It helps if the rice is a bit stickier and not broken up too much. We have basmati and I just serve Safia hers before I stir the rest to fluff it up."
—Farida, mother of Azraa, 2 years, and Safia, 8 months

Risotto

Risotto is a great dish for baby-led weaning. It's one of the easiest ways for babies to eat rice in the early weeks—they pick up soft handfuls of the delicious, creamy rice and push or squeeze it into their mouth. There are many ingredients you can add to a risotto, and the sizes and shapes can be easily adapted to suit your baby. Risotto also sticks well to spoons, allowing your older baby to practice using silverware.

You'll get the best texture using a proper risotto rice, preferably arborio or carnaroli. Add Parmesan cheese and a little butter at the end to help it stick together.

When you are making risotto, the stock should remain hot while you are adding it, so keep it simmering in a pan next to the risotto and add a small ladleful at a time. A traditional risotto needs almost constant stirring, which may be fine when your baby is snuggled up in a sling, or fast asleep, but not so easy if he needs your attention, so we've included an oven-baked alternative. Leftovers (if you have any) can be used to make arancini (see page 62).

Colorful Chicken Risotto

This risotto gives your baby lots of different shapes, flavors, and colors to explore.

Serves 2 adults and 1 baby

1 tablespoon olive oil

2 to 4 tablespoons butter (preferably unsalted)

1 small onion, chopped or sliced

7 to 10 ounces boneless chicken breast or thigh, cut to suit your baby

3¼ cups chicken stock (low-sodium or homemade—see page 176)

1 small red bell pepper, deseeded and cut to suit your baby

1 small zucchini, cut to suit your baby

1 handful corn (canned or frozen) (optional)

¾ cup risotto rice

2 tablespoons grated Parmesan cheese

Freshly ground black pepper, to taste

Heat the oil and butter in a large shallow saucepan. When the butter is melted, add the onion, and fry until soft. Add the chicken and fry gently until the outside is sealed and white.

Meanwhile, put the stock on to heat in a separate pan.

Add the bell pepper and zucchini to the chicken, and fry gently for a further 3 or 4 minutes, until they start to soften, then add the corn (if using). Add the rice and stir to make sure that all the grains have a light coating of the butter/oil mixture (add a little more butter or oil if necessary).

Add the hot stock to the rice mixture, a ladleful at a time, stirring constantly, until each ladleful is absorbed. Simmer gently. Continue adding stock (you may not need all of it) until the rice is plump but still has a "bite," and the overall consistency in the pan is creamy (this will take about 20 to 25 minutes).

Take the pan off the heat, stir in the Parmesan cheese and black pepper, and serve.

Options

• You can use different vegetables, such as peas or mushrooms.
• This dish is also delicious made without the chicken and using vegetable stock instead of the chicken stock.

Mushroom Risotto

This risotto can be made with any type of mushroom, but using large mushrooms (such as portobello) will give your baby a better chance of picking the pieces up individually, if he's just starting out.

Serves 2 adults and 1 baby

3¼ cups chicken stock (low-sodium or homemade—see page 176)

2 tablespoons olive oil

1 small onion, finely chopped

1 garlic clove, finely chopped or crushed (optional)

7 ounces fresh mushrooms, sliced (cremini or portobello are good)

¾ cup risotto rice

Pat of butter (preferably unsalted)

½ cup grated Parmesan cheese

Freshly ground black pepper, to taste

2 tablespoons chopped fresh parsley (optional)

Heat the stock in a saucepan.

Heat the oil in a second, large, shallow saucepan, add the onion, and fry until soft. Add the garlic, and after a few seconds add the mushrooms. Fry for a couple of minutes. Add the rice and stir to make sure that all the grains have a light coating of oil.

Add the hot stock, a ladleful at a time, stirring constantly, until each ladleful is absorbed. Simmer gently. Continue adding stock (you may not need all of it) until the rice is plump but still has a "bite," and the overall consistency in the pan is creamy (this will take 20 to 25 minutes).

Take the pan off the heat and add the butter, Parmesan cheese, and black pepper. Stir well and serve, sprinkled with chopped parsley.

Option

• A few grilled fresh mushrooms make a good topping.

Oven-Baked Eggplant and Zucchini Risotto

This risotto is an easier option if you don't have the time to stand at the stove top stirring and, as with all risottos, your baby will love picking up the soft handfuls of rice. If he still needs stick shapes, the eggplant and zucchini can easily be cut up to suit him.

Serves 2 adults and 1 baby, generously

2½ cups vegetable stock (low-sodium or homemade—see page 177)

2 tablespoons olive oil

1 medium onion, chopped

2 garlic cloves, finely chopped or crushed

1 small eggplant, cut to suit your baby

1 medium zucchini, cut to suit your baby

¾ cup risotto rice

Pat of butter (optional)

1 cup grated Parmesan cheese

Freshly ground black pepper, to taste (optional)

Preheat the oven to 400°F, and heat the stock in a saucepan.

Heat the oil (preferably in a flameproof casserole, so you don't have to transfer the food at the next stage). Add the onion, and fry until soft.

Add the garlic, and after a few seconds add the other vegetables. Cook until they start to soften.

Add the rice and stir to make sure that all the grains have a light coating of oil. Add 2¼ cups stock and bring to a boil.

Cover the dish (or transfer the mixture from the pan to an ovenproof casserole) and put it in the oven to cook for 30 minutes, then stir gently and add more hot stock if necessary. Bake for another 10 minutes.

Remove from the oven and check the texture of the rice; if cooked, add the butter (if using), Parmesan cheese, and black pepper, and stir again.

Cover the dish and leave it to rest for a few minutes before serving.

Mild Vegetable Biryani

This dish is a tasty accompaniment to curries, making a change from plain rice. The rice is soaked before cooking to help the grains stay separate—perfect for when your baby is able to pick up tiny things!

"Sean was so happy when he got the hang of his pincer grip and he could pick up peas. He just loved it—he'd spend ages picking them up really carefully one at a time, and he'd eat loads. He'd be there for ages."

—Pam, mother of Sean, 13 months

Serves 2 adults and 1 baby

⅓ cup basmati rice

1 tablespoon sunflower oil

1 teaspoon cumin seeds

1 large carrot, finely chopped

⅔ cup frozen peas

1 garlic clove, finely chopped or crushed

Pinch of chili powder

Boiling water

> **Tip:** *Mix some thick Greek-style plain yogurt in with the finished dish to make it easier for babies to pick up in handfuls.*

Wash the rice and soak it in a bowl of cold water for about 30 minutes before cooking.

Warm the oil and cumin seeds in a large saucepan (don't allow the seeds to get too brown). Add the drained rice, vegetables, garlic and chili powder, and stir to mix. Pour on boiling water to cover the ingredients by about ½ inch. Cover with a lid, bring back to a boil, and simmer for 10 to 15 minutes, until the water has been absorbed and the rice is plump.

Fluff up with a fork and serve with a curry.

SIDES & VEGETABLES

Babies starting out with solids often have more fun with the sides than the main dish, so it's good to keep them varied to give your baby plenty of new things to try.

Preparing and Cooking Vegetables

All vegetables should be washed in cold water thoroughly before cooking, especially leeks and leafy vegetables, such as loose heads of cabbage, which sometimes have mud between the leaves. If they are not organic it's best to peel root vegetables thinly, as fertilizers and pesticides tend to accumulate in the skin.

Steamed and Boiled Vegetables

Cut your vegetables into pieces of the right shape and size for your baby (see page 19). Try to make sure that vegetables of the same type are cut into pieces that are roughly the same size so that they cook in the same amount of time:

- **Root vegetables**, such as carrots, parsnips, and rutabaga: cut into thick shapes
- **Potatoes**: cut into halves, quarters, or smaller, depending on size; small new potatoes can be cooked whole
- **Leafy vegetables**: shred, tear, or leave whole
- **Broccoli and cauliflower**: cut into florets with some stalk left on
- **Green beans**: trim the ends (topping and tailing) and remove any stringy bits; haricots verts (also called French beans) can be left whole or snapped in half but string beans need to be sliced
- **Brussels sprouts**: trim any ragged leaves and cut a "X" in the bottom of each one (to help them to cook quickly)

Steamed Vegetables

Steaming vegetables retains more flavor, texture, nutrients, and color than boiling. If you don't have a steamer, you can use an ordinary saucepan with a small metal steamer basket or an upturned heat-safe saucer in the bottom. Vegetables can also be "steamed" in a microwave.

Stove-top method: bring some water to a boil in a steamer and cover with a lid for a minute or two. Check that the water is not bubbling into the steamer basket—if it is, empty some water out. Put the vegetables that will take the longest to cook into the steamer first (potatoes and carrots, for example) and put the lid on. Partway through cooking, add the faster-cooking vegetables (preferably in a separate section—if not, just add to the other vegetables, taking care not to overload, as the steam needs to circulate freely).

The cooking time depends on the type of vegetable, how much is in the pan, how small you cut the pieces, and how crunchy you want them. In general, though, hard root vegetables (such as potatoes) take longest; loose green leaves (such as cabbage) cook more quickly. Test with a knife, or by tasting, to check that the vegetables are firm enough for your baby to hold but soft enough for her to munch.

Microwave method: place the prepared vegetables in a microwave-safe bowl with a little water in the bottom. Cover with a loose lid or plastic wrap (pierce a few holes with a skewer or sharp knife). Cooking time will depend on the type of vegetable and how tender you want it to be. Root vegetables, such as potatoes and carrots, take longer to cook, and need to be cooked separately from leafy vegetables.

Approximate cooking times for steaming on the stove top

Spinach/bok choy	1 to 2 minutes
Leafy greens	3 to 5 minutes (they'll turn bright green when cooked)
Broccoli/cauliflower	5 to 10 minutes (test for tenderness)
Green beans	10 minutes (test for tenderness)
Asparagus	10 minutes (test for tenderness)
Carrots	15 minutes (test for tenderness)
Brussels sprouts	15 minutes (test for tenderness)
Corn (on the cob)	15 minutes (test for tenderness)
Yams	20 to 25 minutes (test for tenderness)
Potatoes	20 to 30 minutes (test for softness)

Boiled Vegetables

Although most vegetables are more nutritious steamed, boiling is quicker, and some vegetables, such as frozen peas, tend to taste better boiled. Putting potatoes into cold water, and then bringing it to a boil encourages them to retain less starch; other vegetables (and new potatoes) are best cooked in already boiling water, so that the cooking time is as short as possible and the maximum amount of vitamins is retained.

When the vegetables have been added to the pan, the water should be brought back to a boil, then the pan covered and the vegetables allowed to simmer until they are tender. Cooking times will be slightly less than for steaming; test with a sharp knife when you think they are done. If preferred, vegetables can be cooked in stock (low-sodium or homemade, see page 176) rather than plain water, for extra flavor.

Roasted Vegetables

Roasting vegetables brings out their sweet flavor and makes them easy for babies to grip. It is also a very practical option if you already have the oven on for another dish; most vegetables will roast successfully in an oven set to above or below 400°F, depending on what else you are cooking at the time. Remember, though, that the hotter the temperature, the smaller the pieces need to be—so that the outside doesn't burn before the inside is cooked. The same basic method applies to all types of vegetables, though the cooking time varies. If you need to speed things up, some harder vegetables, such as potatoes, can be parboiled for 5 to 10 minutes before roasting.

Roast Potatoes

Preheat the oven to 400°F. Prepare the potatoes by peeling (or scrubbing) them, then chop into even-sized pieces. Put into a large pan of cold water and bring to a boil. Boil for about 5 to 10 minutes, then drain well using a colander. (Parboiling before roasting makes potatoes nice and crunchy on the outside.)

Give the potatoes a shake in the colander—the more you shake them, the crispier they'll be. Don't overdo it, though, or your baby may not be able to manage them.

Dry the potatoes, then heat enough oil in a small roasting pan to just cover the bottom. Add the potatoes and baste, turn or shake to make sure all surfaces have a thin coating of oil. Check there is a little space around each potato, then roast for about 1 hour (less for small pieces), turning again halfway through.

Potato Wedges

Wedges and slices are easier for small hands to hold and cook more quickly than ordinary roast potatoes. Both sweet potatoes and ordinary potatoes are delicious cooked this way.

Preheat the oven to 400°F. Leave the skins on and cut the potatoes into wedge-shaped segments (or thick slices), putting them into a bowl of cold water as you go. Drain and dry in a clean dish towel.

Heat enough oil in a small roasting pan to just cover the bottom, then add the wedges and baste, turn or shake them to make sure all surfaces have a thin coating of oil. Check that there is a little space around each wedge, then roast them in the oven for about 30 to 40 minutes.

Roasted Winter Vegetables

A good mix of winter vegetables is carrots, parsnips, beets, onion, and squash (or pumpkin).

Preheat the oven to 400°F. Peel, then halve the carrots and parsnips (quarter them if they are very big, but don't cut them too small, because they tend to shrink quite a bit when roasted). Cut any hard core out of the middle.

Peel the beets and onion and cut into chunks.

Leave the skin on the squash (so the pieces keep their shape and your baby can hold them easily) and cut into wedges or chunks.

Heat enough oil in a small roasting pan to just cover the bottom, then add the vegetables and baste, turn or shake them to make sure all surfaces have a thin coating of oil. Check that there is a little space around each piece, then roast for 30 to 40 minutes.

Roasted Summer Vegetables

Eggplant, zucchini, red, orange or yellow bell peppers, tomato, fennel, red onions, and garlic make a tasty roasted vegetable selection. They can be made into a main dish, by stirring them into couscous or pasta, or eaten cold as a salad.

Preheat the oven to 400°F. Leave the skin on the vegetables (except the onion) and cut into pieces of roughly the same size. Zucchini can be halved lengthwise, bell peppers quartered (with the seeds removed), and eggplant, onion, and fennel cut into big chunks. Heads of garlic and tomatoes can be roasted whole.

> **Tip:** *Potatoes can be roasted with other vegetables, but they need to be cut into smaller chunks or wedges to cook in the same time (potatoes should be about half the size of the other vegetables).*

Heat enough oil in a small roasting pan to just cover the bottom, then add the vegetables and baste, turn or shake them to make sure all surfaces have a thin coating of oil. Check that there is a little space around each piece, then roast until tender for 20 to 30 minutes.

> **Tip:** *Try adding herbs, such as rosemary or thyme, to the vegetables before roasting—or for a tangy flavor, marinate them for an hour or so in a mixture of olive oil and balsamic vinegar.*

Broiled Vegetables

Vegetables such as bell peppers, eggplant, zucchini, and tomatoes are delicious broiled, and are perfect for babies who are just starting BLW.

> *"Riley hated steamed zucchini, but he loved it broiled—it was so much nicer, his favorite for ages."* —Cath, mother of Riley, 2 years

Adjust an oven rack to the lowest position for broiling and preheat the broiler. Halve any tomatoes and chop other vegetables into thick strips. Brush them with a little oil, and put them under the broiler.

Turn the vegetables (except the tomatoes) over after about 10 minutes, so that both sides are cooked. Most vegetables will take around 15 to 20 minutes to broil, depending on thickness. Check for tenderness when you think they are done.

Mashed Potatoes and Other Vegetables

Many root vegetables can be mashed, so there's no need to stick to the classic mashed potato. Sweet potatoes, yams, carrot, turnip, and rutabaga are also good, either on their own, mixed with mashed potato (to give some color and a sweeter taste to the potato), or in combinations—carrot with rutabaga, for example.

Steam or boil the vegetables for about 20 to 25 minutes, making sure they are cooked until soft, then drain as necessary.

Mash with a masher, large fork, or hand-held blender, adding a little butter (preferably unsalted) and milk (or cream) as you mash to make it less dry. Add a little ground black pepper to taste. Serve immediately.

Options

- Try adding grated cheese or a finely chopped scallion to mashed potato.
- For extra-creamy mashed potatoes, boil the potatoes in milk instead of water. Use just enough milk to come almost halfway up the potatoes. When they are cooked, mash them with the milk and add a pat of butter.

Couscous

Couscous is very quick and easy to cook and makes a nice change from rice or pasta. Most couscous sold in supermarkets is the "instant" type, which cooks very quickly, just by adding boiling water. (Plain couscous is better than the flavored varieties, as these often have salt added to them.) Authentic couscous needs to be steamed and takes longer. Just follow the instructions on the package of whichever type you buy.

Options

- Try mixing some finely chopped onion or garlic into the dry couscous before adding the water, or stir in some chopped fresh herbs just before serving.
- Add some vegetables, such as strips of roasted bell peppers or steamed beets (chopped or sliced as necessary), to cooked couscous to make a colorful and tasty side dish.

Tip: *To give rice or couscous more flavor, cook it in low-sodium or homemade meat or vegetable stock rather than water.*

Dumplings

Dumplings are an old-fashioned recipe but they are a great way to help your little one to manage soup or stew with her fingers, and they are usually cooked in the same pan.

Makes about 8 dumplings

½ cup all-purpose flour, plus extra for dusting
2 tablespoons very cold butter, grated
1 teaspoon dried mixed herbs (optional)
Pinch of freshly ground black pepper (optional)

Mix together the flour, butter, herbs, and black pepper (if using). Add just enough cold water to hold everything together and mix well to form an elastic dough.

Divide the mixture into about 16 pieces and roll each piece into a ball. Add the balls to the simmering soup or stew for the last 20 minutes of cooking time.

Option

- For extra flavor, add half a small onion (finely grated) and 1 teaspoon chopped fresh thyme, 1 tablespoon chopped fresh parsley or 1 teaspoon caraway seeds.

Homemade Tomato Ketchup

If you like ketchup but don't want to introduce your baby to it because of the large amount of sugar and additives that it usually contains, try this homemade version instead. It will keep for a few days in the fridge or you can freeze it in small quantities.

Makes about 8 ounces

1 cup canned crushed tomatoes

2 teaspoons tomato paste

1 tablespoon cider vinegar

1 garlic clove, finely chopped or crushed

¼ onion, finely chopped

¼ stick of celery, finely chopped

2 cloves

1 bay leaf

Pinch of allspice

Pinch of paprika

Combine all the ingredients in a saucepan and mix well. Bring to a boil and simmer for 5 minutes, stirring occasionally. Remove from the heat and allow to cool.

Remove the cloves and bay leaf and blend the ketchup (with a blender) before serving.

Option
• Try adding some chili powder for a spicier ketchup.

Spicy Tomato Salsa

Spicy tomato salsa goes well with homemade burgers, grilled fish, and chicken. It can also be used to spice up sandwiches and wraps and is great for babies once they can get soft handfuls of food to their mouth. This salsa is best eaten very fresh. (Remember to wash your hands after handling the raw chili pepper, and before touching your baby, because chili juice can sting.)

Makes about 9 ounces

- 2 or 3 large ripe tomatoes (or the equivalent in cherry tomatoes)
- 1 garlic clove
- 2 scallions (or 1 small red onion)
- Approx. 1 teaspoon fresh chili (deseeded and veins removed) or chili flakes (according to taste)
- Juice of ½ lemon (approx. 2 teaspoons) or ½ lime (approx. 2 teaspoons)
- 1 tablespoon olive oil
- 1 or 2 tablespoons chopped fresh parsley or cilantro

Chop the tomatoes, garlic, onions and fresh chili as finely as you can (or use a food processor—but don't let the ingredients turn to mush).

Mix the lemon (or lime) juice and the olive oil in a large bowl. Add the tomato mixture and the parsley or cilantro, and mix well.

Chill for a few minutes before serving.

Option

- Any of the following can be added to a basic spicy tomato salsa: chopped basil; finely chopped cucumber; finely chopped red bell pepper; finely chopped avocado; chopped mint leaves.

DESSERTS

Sweet desserts aren't really essential, but they can be a nutritious part of your family's diet—provided they don't contain large amounts of sugar or artificial sweeteners. Some of the recipes that follow include a little sugar, but they have plenty of other healthy ingredients and are far less sugary than store-bought desserts. Many traditional recipes can be adapted by reducing the amount of sugar or replacing it with fresh or dried fruit. Adding spices, such as cinnamon, can also enhance sweetness.

Although recipes that use cooking apples usually include sugar, you may find that your baby enjoys the natural tartness of the fruit. Alternatively, you can use naturally sweet dessert apples in most recipes, but take care to choose fruit with plenty of flavor.

Of course, the simplest dessert is probably raw fresh fruit, either on its own or with full-fat plain yogurt (preferably with active live cultures), for dipping or eating with a spoon. A range of fruit can give your baby great practice at handling different textures.

Simple Dessert Ideas

Fruit Salad

A fruit salad is best made with fresh, seasonal fruits, but you can add thawed frozen fruit or canned fruit (in its own juice, not in syrup). Wash, peel, and cut the fruit (add bananas at the last minute as they go brown quickly when peeled). A little fruit juice can also be added. Serve as soon as possible. If you need to make the salad in advance, add a dash of lemon juice, cover, and put it in the fridge.

"Liam loves oranges. He'll suck the juice out of a segment, then throw it away, get another segment and keep going until he's had enough."
—Frances, mother of Noah, 2 years, and Liam, 12 months

Natural Fruit Jell-O

It's great fun to watch a baby handling Jell-O! For a sugar-free version all you need is about ¾ ounce powdered or sheet gelatin (vegetarian gelatin is available from health-food stores) and 2 cups pure fruit juice. Prepare the gelatin according to the instructions on the package. Warm the fruit juice in a pan, add the gelatin, and stir until fully dissolved. Pour the mixture into a dish, allow it to cool, then leave it to set in the fridge for a few hours. If you like, you can add pieces of chopped fruit, such as mandarin oranges or pineapple, just before putting the Jell-O into the fridge.

Iced Bananas

These are a great alternative to ice cream. Just peel and mash some ripe bananas and press the mixture into ice popsicle molds or a freezerproof container, then freeze for 3 to 4 hours, until firm. Remove from the freezer and allow to stand for at least 10 minutes at room temperature before serving.

Fruit and Yogurt Popsicles

These make a lovely summer dessert. Just blend about 10 ounces of any fresh, frozen or canned fruit (in its own juice, not syrup) with 18 ounces full-fat thick (Greek-style) plain yogurt. Pour the mixture into ice pop molds and freeze until set. Allow them to stand for 10 minutes at room temperature before eating. If you want a softer popsicle, add around 1 tablespoon of heavy cream to the mixture. Eat within a day or so of making.

Baked Apple Bombs

This is a deliciously sweet dessert and full of goodness. Babies starting out will probably be able to get hold of large pieces of apple, cut into wedges; leave the skin on to make them easier to grip.

Serves 2 adults and 1 baby

Approx. ½ cup apple juice (or a pat of butter, preferably unsalted)

3 firm, sweet or tart apples

4 to 6 dates, pits removed

¼ cup dark or golden raisins (optional)

Pinch of ground cinnamon or nutmeg (optional)

Preheat the oven to 375°F. Pour most of the apple juice into the bottom of an ovenproof dish (or use the butter to grease the dish).

Core the apples (keeping them whole and unpeeled) and place them in the dish.

Fill the centers of the apples with the dates and raisins, and pour the rest of the apple juice over the top.

Sprinkle with cinnamon or nutmeg (if using) and put into the oven. Bake for about 40 minutes, or until the apples are soft.

Serve warm with plain yogurt, crème fraîche, or Homemade Custard Sauce (see page 155).

Options

- You can use pears instead of apples (choose squat round ones rather than long thin ones). Both apples and pears are delicious stuffed with a combination of different dried fruits or, in the summer, fresh fruits such as blueberries or blackberries. One teaspoon of molasses adds extra nutrients and a lovely, rich flavor to the filling— but it's very sticky, so plan your baby's bath time for *after* he's eaten.
- For a similar dish that cooks in less time, use halved apples (or pears, nectarines, or plums), laid facedown on a buttered ovenproof dish and covered in dried fruit, presoaked in a little apple or orange juice.

Warm Apple Wedges

These are great as first foods and dippers for little hands, but they also make a tasty snack or dessert for all ages. Use apples with plenty of flavor.

Serves as many as you wish

1 firm, sweet or tart apple per person
Butter (preferably unsalted) for frying
A few pinches of ground cinnamon (optional)

Peel the apples, cut each one into 8 to 12 wedges and remove the core.

Heat the butter in a frying pan.

Sprinkle the apple wedges with cinnamon, if you like, and fry them very gently for about 15 minutes (depending on initial crunchiness) on all sides, turning as necessary, until just soft.

Lift the wedges onto paper towels to drain and cool slightly.

Serve warm on their own or with Homemade Custard Sauce (see page 155), plain yogurt, or crème fraîche.

Options

- Provided they are not overcooked (when they will be too soft), wedges make good dippers.
- Try mashing the wedges and spreading them on toast.
- Pear wedges also work well, as long as the pear is not too ripe.
- Try adding a few cloves to the butter to give a slightly different spicy flavor.

Rice Pudding

Rice pudding is a lovely, comforting dish that can be made with fruit purée, rather than lots of sugar, making it healthy, too. It's great practice for babies who are learning how to use a spoon, or it can be rolled into balls when cold for younger babies to get hold of.

Serves 2 adults and 1 baby

2 cups milk

¼ cup short-grain rice

2 tablespoons stewed fresh or dried fruit, blended to a purée (apricot, date, fig, and mango are probably the sweetest; you can also use apple, blueberry, blackberry, or pear)

1 teaspoon vanilla extract or 1 vanilla bean

Preheat the oven to 350°F and lightly grease an ovenproof dish.

Pour the milk into a saucepan and bring it to a boil. Stir in the rice and fruit purée and the vanilla extract (if using).

Pour the mixture into the ovenproof dish. If using a vanilla bean, split it open with a knife, scrape out the seeds, and add both the seeds and the bean (don't forget to remove the bean before serving!).

Use a spoon to gently even out the rice throughout the dish. Don't worry that there seems to be very little rice—it expands as it's cooking.

Put the dish into the oven and bake for 15 minutes, then reduce the oven temperature to 300°F and bake for another 60 to 90 minutes, or until the rice has absorbed the milk and the pudding is golden on the top.

Serve warm, perhaps with some stewed fruit, but it is also delicious cold.

Options

- For a richer pudding, replace some of the milk with half-and-half.
- For a traditional rice pudding, replace the fruit purée with 2 tablespoons sugar.
- Try adding ¼ cup raisins or chopped apricots to the mixture before pouring it into the ovenproof dish.
- Swap the vanilla for ½ teaspoon of ground cinnamon, or grate some nutmeg over the surface of the pudding just before it goes into the oven.

Fruit Crumble

This dish works well with any fruit, although apple, peach, blueberry, and strawberry and rhubarb are probably the "classics." Once your baby can get hold of handfuls of food and push or drop them into his mouth, he'll love this.

Serves 2 adults and 1 baby, twice

Butter (preferably unsalted), for greasing
1½ to 2 pounds cooked fruit (see page 156)
¾ cup all-purpose flour
4 tablespoons butter (preferably unsalted)
2 to 2½ tablespoons raw sugar

Preheat the oven to 375°F and lightly grease an ovenproof dish.

Drain the fruit of excess water or juice and place in the ovenproof dish.

Sift the flour into a bowl. Cut or break the butter into small cubes and add it to the flour. Use your fingertips (or a pastry blender or food processor) to rub the butter into the flour until the mixture looks like fine breadcrumbs.

Stir in the sugar, then sprinkle the crumble mixture over the fruit.

Bake in the oven for 25 to 30 minutes, until the top is golden and crisp.

Serve warm or cold, on its own, or with natural yogurt, crème fraîche, or Homemade Custard Sauce (see opposite).

Option

• Spices and/or dried fruit will give added flavor: a handful of raisins and a pinch of nutmeg goes well with apple (although not with strawberry and rhubarb), cloves or a pinch of cinnamon with pears, and ginger with rhubarb. If you prefer to use cooking apples, you may need to add a little sugar to the fruit before baking, depending on taste. Rhubarb and some varieties of plums may also need a little sugar.

Homemade Custard Sauce

This beats custard sauce made from a mix hands down—it's better for you and it tastes better, too. It contains a small amount of sugar but you can reduce this according to what you are serving it with.

1½ cups whole milk

1 vanilla bean, or 1 teaspoon pure vanilla extract

2 large egg yolks

2 teaspoons cornstarch

2 tablespoons granulated sugar

Put the milk into a saucepan and heat gently until the milk is nearly boiling, then take the pan off the heat. Meanwhile, split the vanilla bean with a knife and take out the tiny seeds. Add both the seeds and the bean to the milk.

Whisk the egg yolks with the cornstarch and sugar in a heatproof bowl until the mixture is thick and pale. If you are using vanilla extract, add this now. Pour the milk onto the egg mixture, stirring well. Discard the vanilla bean, if using, and return the mixture to the pan.

Return the pan to low heat and stir continuously until the custard is thick enough to coat the back of a spoon. (This can take up to 8 minutes.)

Serve warm, poured over fruit, such as fresh bananas or peaches, or a sweet dessert such as fruit compote or baked fruit, fruit crumble or fruit pie.

Option

• If you want a more luxurious custard, use heavy cream or half-and-half in place of the milk.

Fruit Compote

Fruit compote makes a great dessert, especially in winter. Most fresh fruit is suitable here; favorites are apples, pears, rhubarb, plums, blackberries (bananas and citrus fruits don't stew well). Dried fruits (such as apricots, prunes, and figs) can also be stewed, but unless they're labeled "ready-to-eat" or "presoaked" they need to be soaked overnight in cold water first. You may want to add about a teaspoon of sugar to some fruit, such as rhubarb, if it is too tart for your taste (although your baby might like it!). Fruits that are very ripe and sweet, and dried fruits, won't need any added sugar.

Note: Fruit should not be cooked in an aluminum or iron saucepan because these metals react with the acid in fruit juice.

Serves 2 adults and 1 baby

1 pound fresh fruit or presoaked dried fruit
¼ cup water
A little sugar, to taste (optional)

Wash, peel, and cut up the fruit as necessary and put it into a saucepan. Add the water and the sugar (if using) and bring to a boil.

Turn down the heat, cover the pan, and simmer until the fruit is soft (anything from 5 to 20 minutes, depending on the fruit). Check occasionally to make sure you can still see some water around the fruit—add more if necessary.

Serve warm or cold, with Homemade Custard Sauce (see opposite), yogurt, crème fraîche, or frozen yogurt. If serving warm, test (by tasting) before offering the fruit to your baby, as some parts may remain very hot.

Options

• Try adding raisins (golden or dark), or nutmeg to apples during the cooking for a warmer flavor; a couple of cloves and a pinch of cinnamon (or a cinnamon stick) works well with pears; cinnamon is also good with plums, and ginger is good with rhubarb.
• You can also cook the fruit in the microwave, in a covered dish with just a few tablespoons of water. It will usually cook more quickly this way.

BREADS & BAKING

Home baking is very satisfying and can be great fun—especially
if you let your toddler help. Home-baked bread and cakes are
much tastier than most store-bought versions, and they avoid the
high salt and sugar levels of most baked goods sold in bakeries,
supermarkets, and cafés.

Bread-Making

Baking your own bread isn't as time-consuming as it sounds, and it gives you the advantage of knowing exactly what is in it, plus the chance to experiment with different ingredients. If you don't have time to knead traditional dough, or to wait for it to rise, you can make a delicious loaf of Easy Bread (see page 160) very quickly.

Your own home-baked bread will almost certainly be healthier than commercial bread—although most people find it's too bland without any salt. For adults, using salted butter or a salty spread will make salt-free bread tastier, but you may want to add up to 1 teaspoon of salt to the recipe (this will also help the bread to keep longer).

The key to baking successfully with yeast is gentle warmth—warm water, warm hands and a warm place for the dough to rise. It's almost impossible to "hurt" dough, so feel free to channel all your energy and frustrations into the kneading—the more vigorous it is, the better.

When shaping your dough, remember that large, solid loaves take longer to cook, and need a cooler oven than small or flat loaves or rolls.

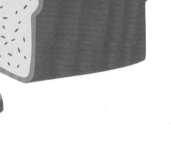

Basic Bread

This recipe is for bread made by hand. You may need to adapt the ingredients (for example, by adding less water) if you are using a breadmaking machine.

Makes 1 large loaf or 12 rolls (see page 160)

1½ teaspoons dried yeast

1 teaspoon sugar

3 cups bread flour (half white and half whole-grain is good), plus extra for dusting

½ teaspoon to 1 teaspoon salt (optional)

1 to 2 tablespoons oil (optional, but it will help the bread to stay moist), plus extra for greasing

1¼ to 1½ cups warm (not hot) water

Sprinkle the yeast and sugar over 1¼ cups of the water, stir to dissolve, and let stand for 5 minutes.

Put the flour and the salt (if using) into a large bowl and make a well in the center. Pour in the oil and add the yeast mixture.

Mix to a smooth, elastic dough, adding more water as necessary. (If it ends up too sticky, just add a little more flour.) A slightly softer mixture is okay for baking in a pan; if you are going to shape the dough on a baking sheet it will need to be slightly stiffer.

Place the dough on a lightly floured surface and knead vigorously for 5 to 10 minutes by pulling the outside of the dough into the center with your fingers, then pushing it out again with your knuckles, and turning it over now and then.

Put the dough back in the bowl, cover it with plastic wrap or a clean, damp dish towel (to prevent a skin from forming) and leave it in a warm place for at least 45 minutes until it has doubled in size and springs back when you press it with a finger.

Lightly grease a large loaf pan or a baking sheet.

Take the dough out of the bowl, punch it a few times to knock out the air, and knead it again for a couple of minutes.

Shape the loaf and put it into the pan or on the baking sheet.

Cover as before and allow to "proof" (i.e. rise for a second time). This usually takes about 20 to 30 minutes. Meanwhile, preheat the oven to 425°F.

When the loaf has risen, put it in the oven and bake for 30 to 40 minutes.

Turn the loaf out to cool on a wire rack.

Alternative Quick Method

If you are in a hurry, you can make bread with just one kneading and rising, although the finished loaf may not be quite as light. Just follow the instructions opposite, then, after one bout of vigorous kneading, shape the loaf and put it into the pan or on the baking sheet. Leave it to rise until it has doubled in size (about 45 minutes) and then put it into a preheated oven.

Options

- You can experiment with different bread flours, such as spelt, or a combination of flours. A loaf made with half white and half whole-grain flour has some of the goodness of the whole wheat but is lighter than whole-grain bread. Ordinary all-purpose flour can be used with reasonable results, but special bread flour works best.
- Using milk instead of water gives a sweeter loaf; using melted butter (preferably unsalted) instead of oil makes it richer.
- Try rolling your loaf in sunflower seeds (or similar small seeds) before the second rising, or sprinkling poppy seeds on top just before baking, to give a crust with extra texture and flavor. (Crush any seeds that may be difficult for your baby to manage before adding them.)
- You can adapt this basic bread recipe to make a variety of tasty loaves or rolls, just by adding extra ingredients when you are mixing the dough. Here are some to try: 1½ cups finely grated cheese and a pinch of freshly ground black pepper; 2 tablespoons sun-dried tomatoes (chopped), with 1 teaspoon dried mixed herbs; 2 tablespoons finely chopped onion; 2 tablespoons crushed sunflower or pumpkin seeds (or poppy or sesame seeds).
- For fruit bread, replace the oil and water with melted (but not hot) butter (preferably unsalted) and warm milk, and add ¼ cup dried fruit, such as raisins, dried apricots (chopped) or cranberries (together with 1 teaspoon ground cinnamon, if you like a spicy flavor). The top can be brushed with warm milk halfway through baking to give a rich, glossy finish.

Storage: Yeast doughs can be kept in the fridge for a few days, or frozen for up to three months. Just punch the air out of the dough after the first rising, wrap it in plastic wrap and put it in the freezer. You will need to bring it back to a warm room temperature before kneading it for the second time and baking it. Baked loaves and rolls (see page 160) can also be frozen, but only for about a month, or the crust will start to break away.

Bread Rolls

Follow the recipe for Basic Bread (see page 158), using slightly less water so that you have a stiffer mixture.

After the second kneading (or the first, if you are in a hurry), lightly grease a baking sheet, then cut the dough into about 12 pieces.

Shape the pieces into rolls and space them at least 2 inches apart on the baking sheet.

Cover with plastic wrap or a clean damp dish towel and leave to proof (rise) until roughly doubled in size.

Heat the oven to 450°F. Bake the bread rolls for about 15 minutes.

Option

• The options at the end of the Basic Bread recipe also work for bread rolls.

Easy Bread

This simple soda bread is quick to make and absolutely delicious, especially fresh from the oven with a little butter. It requires no kneading or rising—the ingredients are simply combined and then popped into the oven, resulting in a lovely rustic loaf.

Makes one 1-pound loaf

1¾ cups all-purpose flour, plus extra for dusting
1¾ cups whole wheat flour
3½ teaspoons baking powder
½ teaspoon baking soda
Pinch of salt (optional)
18 ounces plain yogurt (with active live cultures)

Preheat the oven to 350°F and prepare a floured baking sheet.

Sift the flours, baking powder, baking soda and salt (if using) into a bowl and make a well in the center. Pour in the yogurt and combine with the flour to make a dough, adding a little extra flour if it's too sticky.

Shape the dough into a ball, put it onto the floured baking sheet, and flatten slightly.

Bake in the oven for 50 to 60 minutes, then transfer to a wire rack to cool.

Tortillas and Chapatis

Flat breads, such as Mexican flour tortillas and Indian chapatis, are often easier for babies to handle than breads that have risen. They are usually cooked in a dry pan on the stove rather than in the oven and are very quick to make (most recipes suggest "resting" the dough before cooking, but it's not essential). They're made with all-purpose flour rather than bread flour, and you can use oil or butter instead of the traditional lard.

Makes 10 to 15 tortillas or chapatis

For tortillas: **3 cups all-purpose flour, plus 1 teaspoon baking powder**

For chapatis: **3 cups whole-wheat flour, or half whole-wheat and half white**

A little extra flour for dusting

1 tablespoon lard (unhydrogenated) or butter (preferably unsalted), cut into cubes and softened, or 2 tablespoons oil

1 cup warm water

Sift the flour (and baking powder, for tortillas) into a large bowl and make a well in the center. If using lard or butter, roughly rub it into the flour; if using oil, just mix it straight in. Gradually add 1 cup water (you may not need it all), mixing until the dough holds together. (If it ends up too sticky, just add a little more flour.)

Place the dough on a floured surface and knead for 5 minutes until smooth and springy. Divide the dough into 10 to 15 balls, depending on how large you want your tortillas or chapatis to be. Cover them and allow them to rest for 10 to 15 minutes.

Preheat a large, dry, flat griddle or frying pan over medium–high heat.

Using a well-floured rolling pin and a floured surface, flatten one ball into a thin, round shape, rolling away from you and turning the dough (or the board) once or twice. If you want to use the tortilla/chapati as a wrap, the thinner you get it, the easier it will be to roll up once it's cooked.

Lightly flour the tortilla/chapati and place it in the hot pan. Cook for 45 to 60 seconds until it has a papery feel and the underside is speckled brown, then flip it over and cook the other side for about 30 seconds. As you cook them, stack the cooked breads on a warm plate covered with a clean dish towel to keep them soft. You should just about have time to roll out the next tortilla or chapati while the current one is cooking!

Serve warm or cold, with a filling of your choice, or with a curry or dahl.

Cheese Straws

These delicious, crumbly sticks are great for taking out, and they can be made into the perfect shape and size for your baby to hold—though he will need some practice to discover how to handle them without crushing them. Cheese straws can be eaten on their own or with a dip such as hummus (see page 67).

Makes 12 to 15 straws

4 tablespoons unsalted butter, plus extra for greasing

¾ cup flour, plus extra for dusting

½ cup to ¾ cup cheese, grated

1 egg, beaten

A little cold water (if needed)

Preheat the oven to 400°F and lightly grease a baking sheet.

Put the flour into a bowl. Cut or break the butter into small cubes and add it to the flour. Using your hands, a pastry blender or a food processor, rub the butter into the flour until the mixture looks like fine breadcrumbs.

Stir in the cheese and mix well, then make a well in the center. Pour in the egg and stir until the mixture begins to form a dough, adding a little water, if necessary, to hold it together.

Place the dough on a floured surface and knead it with your fingertips for a few minutes until the ingredients are evenly mixed. Roll the dough into thick pencil shapes 4 to 6 inches long and place them about ¾ inch apart on the baking sheet. Bake for about 10 minutes, until pale golden in color.

Remove from the oven and allow to cool slightly before transferring to a wire rack to finish cooling.

"When Charlie got older and had stopped breastfeeding, his behavior would go downhill mid-morning and mid-afternoon. I didn't realize that he just needed a snack twice a day." —Jan, mother of Charlie, 3 years

English Muffins

Traditional English muffins are slightly richer than bread and make a great alternative to hamburger buns or toast.

Makes about 12 muffins

1 cup milk

1½ teaspoons to 2 teaspoons dried yeast with

1 teaspoon sugar

3 cups bread flour, plus extra for dusting

½ teaspoon to 1 teaspoon salt (optional)

Oil or butter (preferably unsalted) for frying

Put the milk into a pan and heat gently until it is lukewarm. Pour a little into a small bowl and stir in the yeast and sugar.

Sift the flour and salt (if using) into a large bowl and make a well in the center. Pour in the yeast mixture and the rest of the milk, and mix to form a dough. It should feel soft and dry; if it doesn't, add a little more warm milk (to make it softer) or flour (if you need it drier) until you get the right consistency.

Place the dough on a lightly floured surface and knead for about 10 minutes, until it is smooth and elastic. Put the dough back in the bowl, cover it with plastic wrap or a clean, damp dish towel and leave it in a warm place for at least 45 minutes until it has doubled in size and springs back when you press it with a finger.

Take the dough out of the bowl, punch it a few times to knock out the air, and knead it again briefly. Then, using a rolling pin, roll it out to about ½ inch thick.

Using a 3-inch biscuit cutter, cut out as many rounds as you can, kneading the scraps together and re-rolling the dough as needed. Place the muffins on a floured surface and leave them in a warm place for 25 to 35 minutes to rise.

When the muffins are puffy, heat a flat griddle or large frying pan (preferably nonstick), with a very thin coating of oil or butter, over medium heat. Put a few of the muffins on the griddle or into the pan and turn the heat down low. Cook for about 7 minutes, then turn them over and cook for another 7 minutes.

Serve warm, toasted lightly on both sides, then split in half. Spread with unsalted butter and a sweet or savory topping of your choice.

Simple Scones

These simple, egg-free scones are lovely warm or cold. They are quite dense so are easy for younger babies to grasp without crushing. Savory versions go well with guacamole (see page 68), hummus (see page 67), cream cheese, or Bean Spread (see page 69). Plain or fruit scones are great with crème fraîche or whipped cream and jam (or fruit spread).

Makes about 8 scones

1¾ cups all-purpose flour

4 teaspoons baking powder

4 tablespoons butter (preferably unsalted)

½ cup milk

Preheat the oven to 425°F and lightly grease a baking sheet. Put the flour and baking powder together into a bowl. Cut or break the butter into small cubes and add it to the flour. Using your hands, a pastry blender, or a food processor, rub the butter into the flour until the mixture looks like fine breadcrumbs.

Make a well in the center of the mixture and pour in a little of the milk.

Gently fold the dry mixture into the milk and work them together, adding more milk until you have a dough that is soft but not sticky.

On a floured board, knead the dough a little, then roll or gently press it out, so that it is about ¾ inch thick. Cut into round or triangular scones (you can use a biscuit cutter or an upside-down cup for round ones).

Place the scones on the baking sheet, about ¾ inch apart. Bake for 10 to 15 minutes, then cool on a wire rack.

Serve warm or cold.

Options

- Extra ingredients can be added to the mixture, after you've rubbed in the butter and before you add the milk. For fruit scones, try ¼ cup raisins, or chopped dates or dried apricots. For savory scones, try ⅓ cup cooked mashed potato, sweet potato, rutabaga, or butternut squash with ½ teaspoon dried herbs (or 1½ teaspoons fresh herbs).
- For cheese scones, add ½ cup grated cheese.

Muffins

Muffins can be sweet or savory and are usually a big hit with both babies and older children—you'll probably find you are still making them for lunchboxes and picnics when your baby is at school!

A gentle folding technique is used for combining the wet and dry ingredients, as it encourages plenty of air to stay in the mixture, making the muffins nice and light.

Muffins are best baked in a muffin tin. Lining it with paper liners makes the muffins easier to remove and helps to keep them from breaking up when packed to take out with you. The cooking time is approximate—the muffins should be baked until they are golden brown and springy. If you're not sure whether they are done, heat a skewer and gently push it into the center of one of the muffins in the middle of the tin; it should be clean when you pull it out. If there is anything stuck to it, the muffins are not quite ready. If the outside of the muffins begins to burn before the insides are cooked, reduce the temperature of your oven.

The following recipes are for regular-sized muffins, but you may prefer to make smaller ones, so that they are easier for little hands to hold. Smaller muffins will take less time to cook.

Banana Muffins

This tasty sugar-free recipe is a great way to use up bananas that have become a bit too ripe.

Makes 12 regular-sized muffins

1 cup plus 2 tablespoons all-purpose flour (white, whole-wheat, or half of each)

1½ teaspoons baking powder

½ teaspoon ground cinnamon, nutmeg or mixed spice (optional)

4 tablespoons butter (preferably unsalted), plus extra for greasing

4 large, very ripe bananas

2 large eggs, beaten

Preheat the oven to 375°F and lightly grease a muffin tin or line with paper liners.

Sift the flour and spices into a large bowl and make a well in the center.

Melt the butter in a small pan over low heat.

In a separate bowl, mash the bananas to a smooth, thick purée consistency using a fork or a potato masher. Add the eggs and melted butter and mix well.

Pour the banana mixture into the flour and fold together lightly, then spoon the mixture into the muffin tin.

Bake for 10 to 15 minutes (depending on size), until golden brown and springy, then remove from the oven and allow to cool for a few minutes before turning out.

> **Tip:** *Instead of throwing away overripe bananas, put them in the freezer for the next time you make this recipe.*

Option

- If you like, you can add a handful of raisins or finely chopped dates with the banana mixture.

Carrot Muffins

These muffins are surprisingly sweet, and perfect when you want a lighter muffin.

Makes about 10 regular-sized muffins

1 cup plus 2 tablespoons all-purpose flour (white, whole-wheat, or half of each)

1½ teaspoons baking powder

4 tablespoons butter (preferably unsalted), plus extra for greasing

2 large eggs, beaten

2 medium carrots, grated

3 or 4 tablespoons milk

Zest of 2 oranges, juice of 1 (optional)

Preheat the oven to 375°F and lightly grease a muffin tin or line with paper liners.

Sift the flour into a large bowl and make a well in the center.

Melt the butter in a small pan over low heat. In a separate bowl, combine the eggs and grated carrot, then add the melted butter and mix well. Pour the carrot mixture into the flour and fold together lightly.

Add enough milk to give a soft consistency, then spoon the mixture into the muffin tin.

Bake for 10 to 15 minutes (depending on size), until golden brown and springy, then remove from the oven and allow to cool for a few minutes before turning out.

Cheese and Spinach Muffins

Savory muffins make great snacks and are easy for babies to eat.

"Levi doesn't really like sandwiches; he just dismantles them. So we take out savory muffins or cheese scones for a packed lunch or a big snack. They are easy to make and good to freeze, so we've always got some."

—Ruth, mother of Levi, 19 months

Makes 10 regular-sized muffins

Oil or butter (preferably unsalted) for frying, plus extra butter for greasing

½ small red onion, finely chopped

1 cup plus 3 tablespoons all-purpose flour

1½ teaspoons baking powder

1 teaspoon cayenne pepper

1 egg

½ cup milk

⅔ cup grated cheese

2 cups baby spinach leaves, torn

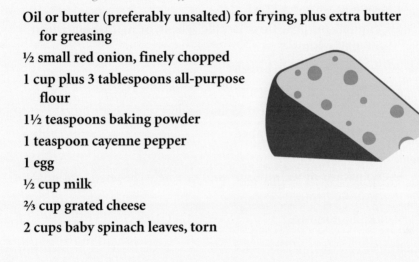

Preheat the oven to 325°F. Heat the oil or butter in a frying pan, add the onion, and fry until soft, then lift it out using a slotted spoon (to drain off the oil) and set aside.

Sift the flour, baking powder and cayenne pepper into a bowl and make a well in the center. Beat the egg in a liquid measuring cup and add the milk, whisking them together, then pour the mixture into the flour and fold together.

Add the cheese, fried onion and spinach, and fold gently until evenly mixed, then spoon the mixture into the muffin tray.

Bake for 15 to 20 minutes (depending on size), until golden brown and springy, then remove from the oven and allow to cool in the muffin tin for a few minutes before turning out.

Morning Glory Muffins

These muffins are delicious, sugar-free and packed with healthy ingredients. Grind the nuts unless you are sure your baby can manage them chopped.

Makes 12 regular-sized muffins

Butter (preferably unsalted), for greasing

2 eggs, beaten

½ cup sunflower oil

1 teaspoon vanilla extract

1½ cups all-purpose flour (whole-wheat, or half whole-wheat and half white)

2½ teaspoons baking powder

2 medium carrots, grated

2 sweet apples, peeled, cored and grated

⅓ cup dates, finely chopped

½ cup dried coconut

½ cup pecans or walnuts, ground or finely chopped (optional)

½ teaspoon ground cinnamon

½ teaspoon nutmeg

Preheat the oven to 350°F and lightly grease a muffin tin or line with paper liners.

Put the eggs, oil, and vanilla into a bowl and mix well. Sift the flour into another bowl and add the carrots, apples, dates, coconut, nuts, and spices. Stir briefly, then make a well in the center. Add the egg mixture and fold together lightly.

Spoon the mixture into the muffin tray and bake for 15 to 25 minutes (depending on size), until golden brown and springy, then remove from the oven and allow to cool for a few minutes before turning out.

Option

• For older children, roughly chopping the nuts will give a lovely texture.

Savory Oat Bars

Oat bars are excellent for picnics and long journeys, being less crumbly and more filling than either scones or muffins. Oats also provide a break from wheat and are very nutritious.

Ordinary quick-cooking oats (not "instant" oats) usually work better for oat bars than rolled oats, which tend to break up when baked and may make the bar too crumbly for your baby to manage easily. A jelly roll pan (approx. 18 × 12 inches and ¾ inch deep) is ideal for making oat bars.

**7 tablespoons butter (preferably unsalted), plus extra for
  greasing**
3 cups rolled oats
2½ cups grated cheese
2 eggs, beaten

Preheat the oven to 350°F and lightly grease a jelly roll pan.

Melt the butter in a small pan over low heat. Remove the pan from the heat and combine all the ingredients in it; mix well. Press the mixture into the greased jelly roll pan using the back of a spoon (it should be about ½ inch thick) and bake in the oven for 20 minutes until golden brown.

Allow to cool in the pan for 5 minutes, then cut into slices and cool on a wire rack.

Option

- You can also add vegetables to this basic recipe, which will give you a lighter bar with varied flavors. Try adding 7 to 10 ounces of one of the following (grated): carrot, zucchini, red onion, sweet potato, rutabaga or parsnip.

Baked Oat Cake

This tasty, moist cake contains no added sugar—the sweetness comes from the fruit and the cinnamon.

> **2 tablespoons oil, plus extra for greasing**
>
> **1 large apple**
>
> **½ cup raisins or other dried fruit**
>
> **A few pinches of ground cinnamon**
>
> **1 or 2 tablespoons water**
>
> **2 cups quick-cooking or rolled oats, pulsed in a food processor to a breadcrumb consistency**
>
> **1 teaspoon baking powder**
>
> **1 cup milk**
>
> **1 egg, beaten**

Preheat the oven to 350°F and lightly grease a 9 × 5-inch loaf pan.

Peel, core and slice the apple and put it into a small saucepan with the raisins, a pinch of cinnamon and the water. Cook gently for about 10 minutes, until the apple is soft, then mash it and mix well with the raisins.

Put all the other ingredients into a bowl and mix well. Add the apple and raisin mixture and combine.

Pour the mixture into the loaf pan and sprinkle cinnamon on the top. Bake in the oven for about 30 minutes. (Insert a skewer to check that it's cooked—it should come out clean.)

Remove from the oven and allow to cool in the pan before turning out and cutting into wedges.

Serve warm or cold, but the cake is easier to cut if allowed to cool first.

Options

- If you want a smoother cake, blend the mixture with an electric mixer before putting it into the loaf pan.
- You can precook the apple and raisins in the microwave, rather than a pan.
- This cake is also delicious with a mashed ripe banana, added along with the apple.

Sugar-Free Carrot Cake

The sweetness in this lovely cake comes from the carrots, dates, coconut, and spices. Grind the nuts unless you are sure your baby can manage them chopped.

1½ cups whole wheat flour

3 teaspoons baking powder

½ cup dates, finely chopped

½ cup coconut

½ cup nuts (e.g. walnuts or mixed nuts), finely chopped or ground

3 teaspoons ground mixed spice, cinnamon or nutmeg

½ cup melted butter (preferably unsalted)

½ cup golden raisins

1 large carrot, grated

Grated zest of 1 orange and 2 tablespoons orange juice

2 eggs, beaten

For the topping (optional):

8 ounces cream cheese (mascarpone also works well)

½ cup dates, finely chopped

Zest and juice of 1 orange or lemon (unwaxed)

Preheat the oven to 300°F and lightly grease a deep 8-inch round cake pan. Sift the flour and baking powder into a large bowl and add the dates, coconut, nuts and spices. Mix thoroughly, then make a well in the center.

Combine the melted butter, raisins, carrot, and orange zest and juice. Add to the dry ingredients and combine to make a thick paste. Add the eggs and mix thoroughly.

Spoon the mixture into the cake pan and place in the oven. Bake for 45 to 60 minutes, or until done. (Check by inserting a skewer—it should come out clean.)

Remove from the oven and allow to cool for 5 to 10 minutes, then turn out onto a wire rack to finish cooling. If using the topping, blend the ingredients until smooth and spread over the cake. Alternatively, serve with mascarpone or whipped cream.

Banana Cake

Banana cake is deliciously moist and sweet. It's best made with bananas that are really overripe—the more they ripen, the sweeter they become, so don't throw those squishy ones away!

Butter or oil for greasing

¾ cup whole wheat flour

2 teaspoons baking powder

½ teaspoon ground pumpkin pie spice

4 tablespoons butter (preferably unsalted)

¼ cup raisins (or chopped figs)

1½ cups mashed banana (1½ or 2 medium-sized ripe bananas)

½ cup walnuts, ground or finely chopped (optional)

1 egg, beaten

For the topping (optional):
8 ounces cream cheese

½ cup 100% fruit spread or jam (optional)

Preheat the oven to 350°F and lightly grease a 9 × 5-inch loaf pan.

Sift the flour into a large bowl and add the spices. Cut or break the butter into small cubes and add it to the flour. Using your hands, a pastry blender or a food processor, rub the butter into the flour until the mixture looks like fine breadcrumbs. Stir in the raisins (or figs) and make a well in the center of the mixture.

In a separate bowl, mash the banana, add the walnuts (if using) and stir in the egg. Pour the banana mixture into the flour mixture and fold in.

Put the mixture into the loaf pan and put it in the oven. Turn the oven down to 325°F and bake for 45 to 60 minutes, or until done. (Check by inserting a skewer—it should come out clean.)

Remove the pan from the oven and allow to cool for 5 to 10 minutes, then turn out onto a wire rack to finish cooling.

Serve plain, with crème fraîche or plain yogurt, or covered with the topping. To make the topping, combine the ingredients and mix thoroughly (using a blender or food processor if the jam is lumpy), then spread evenly over the cake.

Spanish Apple Cake

This delicious, moist cake has plenty of fruit in it and is quick and easy to make, using olive oil rather than butter.

1¾ cups all-purpose flour

3 teaspoons baking powder

½ teaspoon cinnamon

5 tablespoons sugar

Juice and zest of 1 unwaxed lemon

2 eggs, beaten

½ cup plus 2 tablespoons olive oil

1 pound crisp, sweet apples

Preheat the oven to 350°F and lightly grease an 8-inch round cake pan.

Sift the flour and cinnamon into a large bowl and add the sugar and lemon zest.

Make a well in the center and add the eggs, olive oil, and lemon juice, stirring as you go, to make a smooth mixture.

Peel, core, and chop the apples into roughly 1-inch cubes. Fold them gently into the cake mixture and pour everything into the cake pan.

Oven bake for 30 to 40 minutes until firm to the touch in the center and golden brown on top.

Leave the cake to cool slightly in the pan for a few minutes, then turn out onto a wire rack.

Serve cold as a snack, or warm with cream or Homemade Custard Sauce (see page 155).

Option

• You can swap the cinnamon for nutmeg, or use crisp pears instead of apples.

Basic Techniques & Recipes

It's really useful to have a few basic techniques up your sleeve that can be used to make different dishes. Making your own pastry dough, stocks, and sauces will provide the basis of a whole range of meals and means you can choose ingredients that are healthy for your baby.

Pastry Dough

Pastry dough can be made with butter, a mixture of butter and (unhydrogenated) lard, or for a healthier version, olive (or sunflower) oil. The key to making mouthwatering pastry dough is to keep things light and cool, and to handle the dough as little as possible. Use cold water and, if you are making it by hand, try to have cool hands, too. Lifting your hands as you gently rub in the fat will keep the mixture light. If you prefer, you can use a pastry blender or a food processor for the rubbing in, but the kneading, which should be very brief, is best done by hand.

> **Storage:** *Uncooked pastry dough can be kept in the fridge for a couple of days, wrapped in food-safe plastic wrap. Both uncooked and cooked dough freezes well, wrapped tightly.*

When rolling pastry dough (and other doughs), roll away from you, pressing downward more than outward. This will help to keep the dough from shrinking while it cooks. Roll on a floured surface and turn the dough around, so you can keep rolling in the same direction—or use a board and turn the board. There is no need to flip the dough over but you should lift it up occasionally to check that it is not sticking to the board.

Simple Pastry Dough

This recipe makes enough pastry dough to line a 9-inch pie pan; if you want to make a pie with a lid, you will need about 1½ times these quantities.

½ cup fat—butter (preferably unsalted), or half lard (unhydrogenated) and half butter, plus extra for greasing
1¾ cups all-purpose flour, plus extra for dusting
About 3 tablespoons cold water to bind

Lightly grease the pie pan. Put the flour into a bowl and add the fat (cut or broken into small cubes), then use your fingertips to rub the fat into the flour until the mixture looks like fine breadcrumbs. Using a cold blunt knife, stir in the water a few drops at a time with a crisscrossing cutting motion. Stop when the mixture starts to clump together. Gather the mixture into one lump and knead it lightly for a few seconds, using your fingertips only, until it forms a stiff dough.

Place the dough on a lightly floured surface and roll it gently until it is about ⅛-inch thick. Then lift it carefully (by laying it over the rolling pin) and transfer it to your pie pan. Shape the dough to fit, easing it gently into any corners rather than stretching it. Blind-bake the pastry dough (see below) if you like, then fill and cook according to the recipe instructions.

Options

- You can make pastry dough with oil, instead of butter or lard. Olive oil is best for savory dishes, and sunflower oil is better for sweet dishes. Just replace the fat with 5 tablespoons of oil, mixed into the flour with a fork (or electric mixer) until the mixture is crumbly and moist. Gradually add approx. ½ cup cold water, until the mixture starts to clump together, then follow the recipe as above.
- To make cheese-flavored pie crust, use 1½ cups all-purpose flour, 7 tablespoons fat and ½ cup grated cheese. Add the cheese after you've rubbed the fat into the flour.

How to Blind-Bake a Pie Crust

Baking a pie crust "blind" (i.e. with nothing in it) is a way of making sure that the bottom of your pie or quiche doesn't end up soggy. It's especially useful when the filling is very wet or doesn't need to cook for long, so it's good for fruit tarts and quiches.

To keep the bottom of the crust flat and to prevent trapped air from pushing it up, you can either prick the base in several places with a fork, or line it with wax paper and weigh it down with a layer of ceramic pie weights, or dried beans, lentils or rice.

Put the pie crust into an oven preheated to 350°F and cook for 10 to 12 minutes. Check to make sure it's beginning to look dry (but not browned) and remove the weights and paper (if used). If you like, brush the inside with a little beaten egg to keep the crust crisp, then put it back into the oven for another 3 to 5 minutes to finish cooking. Once it's baked, if there are any cracks or holes in the crust, patch them with scraps of raw dough before adding your filling.

STOCKS

A good stock is the basis of many soups, sauces, and other dishes, giving much more flavor to the dish than if you simply used water. Ready-made stock cubes tend to contain a lot of salt, so if you have the time, making your own is a much better option when you have young children. It's also a great way to use "tired" vegetables or the bones from a roast chicken.

Stock is ideal for making in batches and freezing. Large, empty yogurt containers or 1 to 4-cup containers are ideal for this. To use the stock, thaw it in the fridge or put the frozen lump into a pan and bring it to a boil before using it.

Although you can add lots of ingredients and seasonings when you make stock, if you are making it in batches and don't yet know what you are going to use it for, keep it simple and add herbs, garlic, etc., later, according to the eventual recipe.

Simple Meat or Chicken Stock

Meat or chicken stock is made from bones, which are full of flavor. Using a chicken carcass or the bone from a leg of lamb to make stock will mean you get all the goodness out of it (it will also loosen any remaining meat, so you can save that, too). Alternatively, you can buy bones on their own from a butcher specifically for making stock. Ask him or her to chop them into usable-sized pieces for you.

The most basic stock uses just meat bones but you can add a few root vegetables—such as carrots or turnips (but not potato, because it disintegrates when cooked for long periods)—or the stalks of other vegetables, such as broccoli or cauliflower to give a little more flavor.

1 pound meat bones (lamb, beef, pork, or venison), or the
    bones (carcass) from a whole chicken (including any
    remaining skin)

3½ cups cold water

1 celery stick

5 to 10 black peppercorns (optional)

Put the bones into a large stockpot. (If using a chicken carcass, break it up as necessary so that it fits snugly into the pan.) Add 3 to 4 cups cold water, ensuring that the bones are covered, and bring to a boil.

Cut the celery into fairly large pieces. When the water in the pan has boiled, skim any scum off the surface of the liquid, add the celery and peppercorns and bring back to a boil. Skim again if necessary, then reduce the heat, cover, and simmer for about 3 hours.

Strain the stock through a sieve to remove all the solid bits and allow it to cool. Skim off the excess fat, then refrigerate or freeze the stock until you want to use it.

Simple Vegetable Stock

Vegetable stock is made by simmering vegetables until they have given up most of their flavor to the surrounding water. The vegetables are then thrown away. If you want to make a soup that includes vegetables, you will need to use fresh vegetables, rather than those that were used to make the stock. You will need a large stockpot for this recipe.

3 large onions

Approx. 6 medium carrots

4 or 5 celery sticks

1 small turnip

5 to 10 black peppercorns (optional)

Cut the vegetables into fairly large pieces and put into a large stockpot. Add the peppercorns (if using) and 10 cups water and bring to a boil. Reduce the heat, cover, and simmer for about 3 hours.

Strain the stock through a colander to remove all the solid bits and allow it to cool. Refrigerate or freeze the stock until you want to use it.

OTHER BASIC RECIPES

Classic Basil Pesto

Having a jar of pesto in the fridge can be a lifesaver if you are in a hurry—simply cook up some pasta, add pesto and you have a tasty meal. It is also great with fish and adds an extra flavor to soups (add just before serving), sandwiches, roasted vegetables and many other dishes.

Most store-bought versions of pesto contain salt, but it's easy to make your own and it keeps well in the fridge. This is a very tasty version, with a good texture; it can be made in a mortar and pestle (if you want to be traditional), or in a food processor (if you're in a hurry).

The amounts of cheese, pine nuts, and oil can be varied according to taste. It's probably best to avoid Chinese and Korean pine nuts as these can occasionally leave a bitter aftertaste.

1 large bunch fresh basil

1 or 2 garlic cloves, finely chopped or crushed

¼ cup pine nuts

1 cup freshly grated Parmesan cheese

½ cup freshly grated Pecorino cheese (or another ½ cup Parmesan)

7 tablespoons olive oil

Pinch of ground black pepper (optional)

Mortar and Pestle Method

Roughly chop the basil leaves and pound in a large mortar with the chopped garlic.

Crush the pine nuts between sheets of waxed paper with a rolling pin (optional, but it saves time). Add the pine nuts to the mortar and grind the mixture thoroughly until you have a thick paste.

Add the cheeses and pound again. Add the olive oil a little at a time, testing for preferred texture, then add a pinch of black pepper if desired, and grind or pound again.

Allow the pesto to stand for 5 minutes before serving.

Food Processor Method

Combine the basil, garlic, and cheese and blend.

Add the nuts and blend again briefly.

Keep blending and slowly add the olive oil, checking the consistency as you go. Don't aim for complete smoothness—it should have some texture. Transfer the mixture to a bowl and add black pepper to taste.

Allow the pesto to stand for 5 minutes before serving.

Options

- For an extra-nutty flavor, toast the pine nuts slightly beforehand by warming them for a few minutes in a dry frying pan.
- If you like, you can use walnuts or cashew nuts instead of pine nuts.
- Add a little lemon juice at the end, for an extra kick.
- You can use arugula—or even watercress—instead of basil.

Quick Curry Paste

This basic mild curry paste will keep in the fridge for a couple of weeks. It's made with ready-ground spices, but, if you have a spice grinder (or a large mortar and pestle and plenty of time), you can start with whole coriander and cumin seeds for a more authentic version. (Remember to wash your hands after handling the raw chili pepper and before touching your baby, because chili juice can sting.)

1 fresh mild/medium chili pepper (deseeded, veins removed), finely chopped

5 or 6 garlic cloves, finely chopped or crushed

¾-inch piece of fresh ginger, grated

4 tablespoons ground coriander seeds

4 tablespoons ground cumin seeds

2 tablespoons mustard seeds, crushed

1 tablespoon chili powder

1 tablespoon turmeric

1 tablespoon paprika

Olive oil

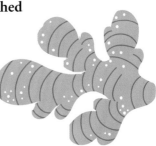

Finely chop the chili pepper. Add the garlic and ginger (and any juices) and grind until fairly smooth. Add the spices and grind again. Add enough oil to make a soft paste.

Transfer the paste to a jar and put it in the fridge.

Mild Thai Green Curry Paste

Recipes such as Thai green fish or chicken curry call for Thai green curry paste. Store-bought varieties tend to be very hot, as do many recipes for homemade versions. This is a milder version but it's still quite hot, so you may want to offer your baby a tiny amount and include plenty of mild coconut milk in your curry to start with. Alternatively, you could use a little less chili pepper. The paste will keep for about a week in an airtight jar in the fridge. (Remember to wash your hands after handling the raw chili pepper and before touching your baby, because chili juice can sting.)

> 2 mild/medium green chili peppers (deseeded and veins removed)
>
> 2 shallots (or 4 scallions)
>
> 3 garlic cloves
>
> 1-inch piece of fresh ginger, peeled
>
> 2 lemongrass stalks, trimmed, outer leaves discarded and chopped
>
> 2 tablespoons fresh chopped cilantro
>
> 1 teaspoon ground cumin
>
> 1 teaspoon ground coriander seeds
>
> 1 teaspoon grated lime zest (unwaxed)
>
> 1 tablespoon lime juice
>
> 2 tablespoons oil (if needed)

Finely chop the chili peppers, shallots, garlic, and ginger by hand or using a food processor. Add the other ingredients and blend thoroughly until smooth (use a mortar and pestle for a really smooth paste). Add a little oil, if needed, to give a manageable consistency.

White Sauce and Variations

White sauce is the basis for many sauces, used in dishes such as lasagna and fish pie. The roux method is the "classic" way to make a white sauce, but the cornstarch and microwave methods are both quicker.

The Roux Method

2 tablespoons butter (preferably unsalted)
3 tablespoons all-purpose flour
1½ cups milk

Melt the butter in a saucepan, add the flour and stir to make a paste (the roux). Cook gently for 2 or 3 minutes until the roux starts to bubble.

Remove the pan from the heat and add a little of the milk. Stir (with a spoon or a whisk) until the mixture is smooth. Gradually add the rest of the milk, stirring or whisking all the time to prevent lumps forming. Return the pan to the heat and bring to a boil, still stirring.

Keep the sauce just about at boiling point (and keep stirring) until it has finished thickening, plus another 1 or 2 minutes, to make sure it's completely cooked.

The Cornstarch Method

1½ cups milk
2 tablespoons cornstarch

Put almost all the milk (except for 2 or 3 tablespoons) into a saucepan and bring to a boil. Meanwhile, in a small bowl, mix the remaining milk with the cornstarch to make a smooth cream. When the milk is boiling, pour a little of it into the cornstarch mixture and stir well.

Pour the cornstarch mixture into the remaining milk and bring to a boil, stirring (with a spoon or a whisk) all the time to prevent lumps from forming. Keep the sauce just about at boiling point (and keep stirring) until it has finished thickening, then cook for another 1 or 2 minutes, to make sure it's completely cooked.

> **Tip:** *Cornstarch blended with a little cold water or milk can be added to any sauce that needs thickening.*

The All-in-One Microwave Method

2 tablespoons butter (preferably unsalted)
3 tablespoons all-purpose flour
1½ cups milk (at room temperature or lukewarm)

Put the butter into a microwaveable bowl and heat it in the microwave for 20 to 40 seconds on HIGH until melted. Remove from the microwave and add the flour and milk. Whisk together vigorously.

Cook on high for 2 to 4 minutes, stopping every 30 seconds to whisk again, until the sauce is thick and thoroughly hot. Give it a final whisk before serving.

Options

• When making a savory sauce, you can replace up to half the milk with stock.
• If you want a thinner sauce, add a little more milk, stock, or water at the end.

Variations on Plain White Sauce

Once you can make a plain white sauce you'll find it easy to adapt the recipe to create more interesting sauces.

Béchamel Sauce
This sauce is often used in lasagnas and the Greek dish moussaka. Make the white sauce as on page 181, using a little less milk for a thicker consistency. Add a little grated nutmeg to finish.

Cheese Sauce
Make the white sauce as on page 181, then remove from the heat and stir in ½ cup to ¾ cup grated cheese (depending how cheesy you want the sauce to be). (Don't keep cooking it, or the cheese may go stringy.) Add 1 teaspoon mustard with the flour or cornstarch for extra flavor.

Fish Sauce
For a sauce to serve with poached fish, use only ½ cup milk for the sauce (so that it is very thick), then, once the fish is cooked, stir ½ cup of the poaching liquid into the sauce.

Further Information

The following online discussion forums have a particular focus on baby-led weaning:

www.babyledweaning.com/forum/
http://groups.yahoo.com/group/B-LW/
The baby-led weaning group on www.facebook.com

About the Authors

Gill Rapley has studied infant feeding and child development for many years. She worked as a public health nurse for more than 20 years and has also been a midwife and a breastfeeding counselor. She developed the theory of baby-led weaning while studying babies' developmental readiness for solids as part of her master's degree. She lives in Kent, England, with her husband and has three grown children, all of whom tried their best to show her that they didn't need any help with solid foods.

Tracey Murkett is a writer and journalist. After following baby-led weaning with her daughter, she wanted to let other parents know how easy and stress-free mealtimes with babies and young children can be. She lives in London with her partner and their five-year-old daughter.

Their first book, *Baby-Led Weaning: The Essential Guide to Introducing Solid Foods— and Helping Your Baby to Grow Up a Happy and Confident Eater*, has inspired many families to follow baby-led weaning.

Acknowledgments

We would like to thank the many parents who sent us their thoughts, recipes, and photos, as well as the administrators and members of the online forums who helped to generate such an enthusiastic response. Thanks also to our small army of recipe testers and to Philippa Davis of Mudchute Kitchen, London, for the Easy Bread recipe.

Special thanks go to Carol Williams (of the Infant Feeding Consortium and the Institute of Child Health, University of London) for nutritional advice, to Judith Bird, Jessica Figueras, Lydia Hoult, Elizabeth Mayo, Derrick Murkett, and Sarah Squires for providing their insights on the manuscript, and to our agent, Clare Hulton, and our editors, Julia Kellaway and Louise Coe, for their patience. And, of course, huge thanks to our partners and families, for their long-suffering support.

Index